First World War
and Army of Occupation
War Diary
France, Belgium and Germany

51 DIVISION
152 Infantry Brigade
Gordon Highlanders
6/7th Battalion
1 March 1918 - 31 March 1918

WO95/2868/2

The Naval & Military Press Ltd
www.nmarchive.com
Published in association with The National Archives

Published by

The Naval & Military Press Ltd

Unit 10 Ridgewood Industrial Park,

Uckfield, East Sussex,

TN22 5QE England

Tel: +44 (0) 1825 749494

www.naval-military-press.com

www.nmarchive.com

This diary has been reprinted in facsimile from the original. Any imperfections are inevitably reproduced and the quality may fall short of modern type and cartographic standards.

© **Crown Copyright**
Images reproduced by permission of The National Archives, London, England, 2015.

Contents

Document type	Place/Title	Date From	Date To
Heading	WO95/2868-2 6/7 Bn Gordon Highlands Oct 1918-Mar 1919		
Heading	51 Division 152 Bde 6/7 Bn Gordon Highlanders 1918 Oct-1919 Mar		
Miscellaneous	War Diary Of 6/7th Battalion The Gordon Highlanders To Period 1st October 1918 31st October 1918 Volume 48		
War Diary	Railway Embankment	01/10/1918	02/10/1918
War Diary	Frevin Capelle	03/10/1918	06/10/1918
War Diary	Queant	06/10/1918	10/10/1918
War Diary	Bourlon	11/10/1918	11/10/1918
War Diary	Iwuy	12/10/1918	12/10/1918
War Diary	Avesnes-Le-Sec	12/10/1918	14/10/1918
War Diary	Iwuy	15/10/1918	16/10/1918
War Diary	Thun St. Martin	17/10/1918	20/10/1918
War Diary	Lieu St Amand	20/10/1918	21/10/1918
War Diary	Novelles	22/10/1918	24/10/1918
War Diary	Maing	25/10/1918	28/10/1918
War Diary	Neuville-Sur-L'Escaut	29/10/1918	29/10/1918
War Diary	Thun Leveque	30/10/1918	31/10/1918
Miscellaneous	Received In Front Line	14/10/1918	14/10/1918
Miscellaneous	51 (H) Div. Signal School	11/10/1918	11/10/1918
Miscellaneous	A Form Messages And Signals.		
Miscellaneous	Narrative Of Operations	02/11/1918	02/11/1918
Miscellaneous	Headquarters 152nd Infantry Brigade	19/10/1918	19/10/1918
Operation(al) Order(s)	Operation Order No. 212	02/10/1918	02/10/1918
Miscellaneous	Administrative Instructions	02/10/1918	02/10/1918
Operation(al) Order(s)	The Gordon Highlanders Operation Order No. 213	05/10/1918	05/10/1918
Operation(al) Order(s)	The Gordon Highlanders Operation Order No. 215	11/10/1918	11/10/1918
Operation(al) Order(s)	The Gordon Highlanders Operation Order No. 215	10/10/1918	10/10/1918
Miscellaneous	Administrative Instructions Issued In Conjunction With O.O No.215	10/10/1918	10/10/1918
Operation(al) Order(s)	The Gordon Highlanders Operation Order No. 215	10/10/1918	10/10/1918
Map	Map		
Operation(al) Order(s)	6/7 Bn Gordon Highlanders Operation Order No. 216	14/10/1918	14/10/1918
Miscellaneous	Administrative Instructions	14/10/1918	14/10/1918
Operation(al) Order(s)	The Gordon Highlanders Operation Order No. 217	17/10/1918	17/10/1918
Operation(al) Order(s)	The Gordon Highlanders Operation Order No. 218	20/10/1918	20/10/1918
Operation(al) Order(s)	The Gordon Highlanders Operation Order No. 219	21/10/1918	21/10/1918
Operation(al) Order(s)	The Gordon Highlanders Operation Order No. 220	24/10/1918	24/10/1918
Operation(al) Order(s)	The Gordon Highlanders Operation Order No. 224	30/10/1918	30/10/1918
Heading	War Diary Of 6/7th Battalion The Gordon Highlanders For Period 1st November 1918 30th November 1918 Volume 49		
War Diary	Thun Levecque	01/11/1918	30/11/1918
Heading	War Diary Of 6/7th Battalion The Gordon Highlanders From 1st To 31st December 1918 (Volume 50)		
War Diary	Thun Leveque	01/12/1918	31/12/1918
Map	Map		
War Diary	Thun Leveque	01/01/1919	06/01/1919

War Diary	Houdeng Aimeries	07/01/1919	31/01/1919
Heading	War Diary Of 6/7th Battalion The Gordon Highlanders For Period 1st February 1919 28th February 1919 Volume 52		
War Diary	Houdeng Aimeries	01/02/1919	31/03/1919
War Diary	Fremicourt	01/03/1918	01/03/1918
War Diary	In Trenches	02/03/1918	07/03/1918
War Diary	O'Shea Camp	08/03/1918	18/03/1918
War Diary	In Trenches	19/03/1918	26/03/1918
War Diary	Neuvillette	27/03/1918	28/03/1918
War Diary	Neuvillette-Labeuvriere	29/03/1918	29/03/1918
War Diary	Labeuvriere	30/03/1918	31/03/1918
Miscellaneous	Account Of Operations Commencing Near Boursies	31/03/1918	31/03/1918
War Diary	Fremicourt	01/03/1918	01/03/1918
War Diary	In Trenches	02/03/1918	07/03/1918
War Diary	O'Shea Camp	08/03/1918	18/03/1918
War Diary	In Trenches	19/03/1918	26/03/1918
War Diary	Neuvillette	27/03/1918	28/03/1918
War Diary	Neuvillette-Labeuvriere	29/03/1918	29/03/1918
War Diary	Labeuvriere	30/03/1918	31/03/1918
Miscellaneous	Account Of Operations Commencing Near Boursies	31/03/1918	31/03/1918
War Diary	Fremicourt	01/03/1918	01/03/1918
War Diary	In Trenches	02/03/1918	07/03/1918
War Diary	O'Shea Camp	08/03/1918	18/03/1918
War Diary	In Trenches	19/03/1918	26/03/1918
War Diary	Neuvillette	27/03/1918	28/03/1918
War Diary	Neuvillette-Labeuvriere	29/03/1918	29/03/1918
War Diary	Labeuvriere	30/03/1918	31/03/1918
Miscellaneous	Account Of Operations Commencing Near Boursies	31/03/1918	31/03/1918
Heading	War Diary Of 6/7th Battalion The Gordon Highlanders For Period 1st January 1919 31st January 1919 Volume 50		

② WO95/2868 6/7 Bn Gordon Highlanders Oct 1918 – Mar 1919

51 DIVISION

152 BDE

6/7 BN GORDON HIGHLANDERS

1918 OCT - 1919 MAR

No 48 152/51

CONFIDENTIAL

War Diary

of

6/7th Battalion, The Gordon Highlanders

For Period

1st October 1918 to 31st October 1918.

Volume 48.

(6392) Wt. W6192/P875 1,500,000 4/18 McA & W Ltd (E 2815) Forms W3091/4.   Army Form W.3091.

Cover for Documents.

Nature of Enclosures.

Notes, or Letters written.

Army Form C. 2118.

WAR DIARY
or
INTELLIGENCE SUMMARY.
(Erase heading not required.)

Instructions regarding War Diaries and Intelligence Summaries are contained in F. S. Regs., Part II. and the Staff Manual respectively. Title pages will be prepared in manuscript.

Place	Date	Hour	Summary of Events and Information	Remarks and references to Appendices
RAILWAY EMBANKMENT.	1.10.18.		Weather very fine and bright. All Companies carrying out P.T., Box Respirator drill, musketry, rifle exercises, digging etc. One platoon of "C" Coy employed on salvage forward of CAROLINE Trench; other platoons of "C" Coy carrying out Bombing and Rifle Grenade practice. News all along the line very good.	OO.2/2
	2.10.18.		Weather very fine and bright. All companies employed on cleaning kit & billets etc. prior to moving back to FREVEN CAPELLE area with Battalion H.Q. at the Mairie, FREVEN CAPELLE. The move was carried out by buses, and the Embussing Point was at ATHIES Cross-roads, H.14.d.95.05, time 16.00 hours and Lieut. BLACK and 1 N.C.O. "B" Coy were at Embussing Point at 15.00 hours and marked lorries off by Companies. Lieut. J.L. Hay and 1 N.C.O. per Company reported at CULLINGWOOD CAMP at 09.00 hours; they were conveyed to FREVEN CAPELLE and reported to Area Commandant for accommodation. The personnel left at Transport Lines, ECURIE, moved by march route. Battalion actually left ATHIES CROSS-Roads at 17.30 and arrived at FREVEN CAPELLE at 20.50, where a hot meal awaited the men. The Companies on departure from the Railway Embankment were played out by the band of the 2nd DEVONS, the regiment which relieved the 6th Gordons. Just before the battalion was relieved, the weather changed and light rain fell.	
FREVIN CAPELLE.	3.10.18.		Weather fine. The Commanding Officer inspected the billets of all Coys. "A" and "B" Coys billeted in houses in village 1½ kilometres from FREVEN CAPELLE; "C" Coy accommodated in Huts; "D" Coy billeted in houses in FREVEN CAPELLE. Headquarters Details in tents and billets. News from line generally good.	
	4.10.18.		Weather fine but cloudy. Companies carrying on with arm drill, box Respirator drill, preliminary musketry and platoon in attack. Commanding Officer visited all billets. News from front still good.	

Army Form C. 2118.

WAR DIARY
or
INTELLIGENCE SUMMARY.
(Erase heading not required.)

Instructions regarding War Diaries and Intelligence Summaries are contained in F. S. Regs., Part II. and the Staff Manual respectively. Title pages will be prepared in manuscript.

Place	Date	Hour	Summary of Events and Information	Remarks and references to Appendices
FREVIN CAPELLE	5.10.18.		Weather fine but overcast. The battalion was amalgamated with the 7th Gordon Highlanders to-day and will henceforth be known as the "6/7th Gordon Highlanders". The change of designation to take effect from midnight 5th/6th October 1918. Companies carried out Musketry, Platoon and Company in Attack under the Platoon and Company Commanders. Companies went to Baths at ECOIVRES in afternoon. Battalion received Warning Order re move to East of CAMBRAI. Received notification that Winter Time will come into use at midnight to-night; clocks being put back one hour, and for purposes of Field and Signal messages, the time will run on to 24.59 hours on 5th October and will then change to 00.01 hours on 6th October.	OO.2.13
QUEANT	6.10.18.		Advance party under Lieut. FREVIN CAPELLE at 07.30 hours. Transport left for new camp at same time. Commanding Officer visited all Companies and found billets in perfectly clean condition and ready to evacuate. Orders received that all surplus personnel over 900 other ranks are to be sent to Divisional Reception Camp to-day. O. C. Coys ordered to detail seven other ranks each. Pipers and Drummers, attached Battalion H⁀., are also to parade with this party. 2/Lieut. ALEXANDER to conduct party to Reception Camp and return to Battalion on completion of duty. Orders were issued for O.C.Coys to hold kit inspection of men arrived from 7th Battalion, Gordon Highlanders, and all deficiencies are to be notified to Orderly Room by 15.30 hours to-day. The Commanding Officer held inspection of 7th Gordon Highlanders sent to 6th Battalion Gordon Highrs. in connection with Amalgamation. Battalion left FREVIN CAPELLE by buses from ARRAS - ST.POL Road at 18.40 and arrived at destination at 22.20 hours, Canadian Corps Area "D", and took over from the 12th Canadian Infantry Brigade in C.6.b. and a., 1500 yds North West of QUEANT. The 6/7th Gordon Highrs. took over from the ---- 38th Canadian Infantry Battalion. Bosche aeroplane dropped several bombs whilst men were proceeding to their billets and resulted in several casualties. Captain P.M.McKENZIE and five men were killed and thirty-eight wounded. Weather cloudy and a light rain fell in the afternoon.	

Army Form C. 2118.

WAR DIARY
or
INTELLIGENCE SUMMARY.

(Erase heading not required.)

Instructions regarding War Diaries and Intelligence Summaries are contained in F. S. Regs., Part II. and the Staff Manual respectively. Title pages will be prepared in manuscript.

Place	Date	Hour	Summary of Events and Information	Remarks and references to Appendices
QUEANT.	7.10.18.		Battalion camped in trenches and dug-outs; "D" Coy in dugouts in SUNKEN ROAD; "A", "B" and "C" Coys and Headquarters in trenches. The Commanding Officer visited all Companies and ordered dug-outs to be cleaned and new latrines dug, one per Company. Funeral of Captain F.McKenzie and 5 men to QUEANT Cemetery.	
	8.10.18.		All Companies on cleaning kit during morning. During the afternoon all men were engaged on Salvage work. The Commanding Officer, Adjutant, Major Cran and Captain Paterson proceeded in the direction of BOURLON WOOD but owing to the lateness of the hour, they were only able to reach INCHY and MOEUVRES. Weather rainy during the morning, and unsettled during the afternoon.	
	9.10.18.		Weather very fine. General SEGRAVE visited lines and inspected men's accomodation. Orders received to hold the battalion in readiness to move at an hour's notice. Companies carrying out Box Respirator drill and Company in attack. Orders received for Battalion to proceed to BOURLON, passing Starting Point at 11.30 hours to-morrow. News received of the fall of CAMBRAI, and the Bosche retreating rapidly beyond it.	
	10.10.18.		Battalion left QUEANT for BOURLON, passing Starting Point at 11.30 and reached BOURLON at 16.45 hours. All Coys received hot meal on arrival. Headquarters billeted in a Chateau, and Companies in dug-outs and shacks in BOURLON WOOD. Weather fine. News from front continues to be very good. Bosche reported to be retreating well beyond CAMBRAI.	

Army Form C. 2118.

WAR DIARY
or
INTELLIGENCE SUMMARY.
(Erase heading not required.)

Instructions regarding War Diaries and Intelligence Summaries are contained in F. S. Regs., Part II. and the Staff Manual respectively. Title pages will be prepared in manuscript.

Place	Date	Hour	Summary of Events and Information	Remarks and references to Appendices
				OO. 215
BOURLON.	11.10.18.		The battalion left BOURLON by march route to relieve the 21st CANADIAN Infantry Battalion, 4th Brigade, at 12.30 and passed Starting Point at 13.00 hours and arrived at ESCAUDOEUVRES at 17.00. Considerable blockage of the road was experienced and long delays occurred. At 19.15 hours the battalion moved up to take over front line. Colonel THOM went on in advance and Major CRAN and Lieut. COLLIER brought on battalion and at 02.30 hours on the morning of the 12th Oct., the battalion arrived at the front line positions and proceeded to carry out the relief which was completed at 03.30 hours. Echelon "B" established at T.20.b.2.1.	
IWUY. AVESNES-le-SEC.	12.10.18.		Battalion went into position along Road at 03.30 and at 10.00 went into action with objective: Road from O.8.c.8.3 to O.15.c.9.3. The advance was met with very little opposition, and with only about 30 casualties, of which mostly all were slight, and objective was reached by 12.00. The main line of resistance was formed at Road from O.8.c.8.3 to O.15.c.9.3, and the Companies there dug in; Support Line was formed along at rear of Mill at O.15.c.2.0 to O.21.a.8.7. Captain RISK reported in off leave at Echelon "B". Battalion H.Q. established in MOULIN de PIERRE.	
AVESNES-le-SEC.	13.10.18.		After artillery bombardment, the battalion attacked with objective in view Wood and Railway directly in front. Severe opposition was met by machine gun fire from Wood and Railway. At 10.30 the battalion the forced to retire back to the original jumping-off point from O.8.c.8.3 to O.15.c.9.3. which owing to the severe fire from enemy machine guns was only reached at 12.00. At 03.30 Colonel THOM was wounded whilst taking observations on the top of the MOULIN de PIERRE. Major CRAN and Captain RISK were ordered up from Echelon "B". Colonel LAWRIE given command of all the front line battalions, viz - 4th and 5th Seaforths and 6/7th Gordons. During this day the battalion suffered heavy casualties; Lieut. Henderson being killed and 7 other officers being wounded (Captain REID severely) and 22 men killed and 271 men wounded and gassed, 17 missing and 4 died of wounds.	

WAR DIARY
or
INTELLIGENCE SUMMARY.

(Erase heading not required.)

Army Form C. 2118.

Place	Date	Hour	Summary of Events and Information	Remarks and references to Appendices
AVESNES-le-SEC.	14.10.18.		Our artillery heavily bombarded the Wood and Railway from 08.00 until 09.00 and from 09.30 till 10.00, after which we sent out a patrol of 20 men to reconnoitre Wood, and at same time 5th Seaforths sent out a patrol of 20 men and 1 Officer to reconnoitre the Railway, with the object in both cases of reporting on enemy strength at those two points where the attack had been held up yesterday. At 11.30 word was brought back by one of our patrol to the effect that our patrol had found the enemy in great strength in machine guns and that the patrol had gone right through the wood and got as far as the house at about O.15.b.3.3, which was an absolute nest of machine guns which opened fire on them; they retired through wood to return to our lines but were held up at point O.9.c.7.3 again by severe M.G. fire and snipers. This man, who by the way volunteered to find his way to us, reported that if possible the patrol would try to get back before night but, if not, they would return at dusk. At 16.30 Serge at STABLES reported to Headquarters to the effect that the patrol had got back but in doing so 2 men were killed and 3 wounded. This NCO's report was very clearly given, accurate and of great value. At 19.00 hours, the battalion was relieved in the front line by the 6th Seaforths. During the early part of the evening, the enemy put over a good deal of BLUE and YELLOW CROSS GAS. Received report of death (from wounds) of Captain A.REID of "C" Company. Weather during the day fine and clear. Battalion moved back to Sunken Road at O.31 and men settled down in Cubby-holes; men had hot meal on arrival here. During the night enemy shelled this area severely with H.V. and BLUE & YELLOW CROSS GAS.	A OO.216
IWUY	15.10.18.		Battalion in Sunken Road at O.31.c & d. and remains in Reserve here; men busy cleaning up and resting. During early hours of morning, also afternoon and evening, enemy heavily shelled this area. "D" Coy was taken into IWUY & billeted there. All Coys had baths to-day at "D" Coy's billet in IWUY. Enemy still shelling this area.	

Army Form C. 2118.

WAR DIARY
of
INTELLIGENCE SUMMARY.
(Erase heading not required.)

Instructions regarding War Diaries and Intelligence Summaries are contained in F.S. Regs., Part II. and the Staff Manual respectively. Title pages will be prepared in manuscript.

Place	Date	Hour	Summary of Events and Information	Remarks and references to Appendices
IWUY.	16.10.18.		Weather rainy and dull. "A", "B" & "C" Coys still in Sunken Road, "D" Coy at IWUY. Enemy guns still very active shelling this area, a good deal of BLUE and YELLOW CROSS Gas put over and, in spite of enemy precaution being taken, a few men were gassed. Our batteries very active shelling Wood and Railway and enemy's rear areas. One of our men ("B" Coy) who had been wounded on the 14th Oct. near the Wood, crawled into our lines in a very exhausted condition; he was taken to Aid Post where he soon revived considerably. He confirmed the report of our patrol of the 14th as regards enemy machine guns in the Wood, he having been wounded just at the front edge of this Wood.	'B'
THUN- ST.MARTIN.	17.10.18.		Battalion was relieved from the Reserve by the 4th Seaforths and moved by march route to THUN ST.MARTIN, where the men were billeted and settled down by 17.00 hours. They received a good hot meal on arrival in this new area. Echelon "B" joined Battalion here. The 154 Inf.Bde. relieved the 152 Inf.Bde. Colonel CRANSTOUN reported from leave and took command of the Battalion.	00217
	18.10.18.		Commanding officer inspected billets during morning, as also did General SEYRAVE. Billets were found to be very dirty, and men were employed all day cleaning same. Report of capture of OSTEND and BRUGES received. Commanding Officer held conference with Coy Commanders at 12.00 hours & settled all points reference re-organisation of Companies &c. Weather dull and threatening rain; misty.	
	19.10.18.		Battalion still quartered at THUN ST.MARTIN. All Coys had inspections under Coy Commanders - kit, equipment & feet. All Coys well employed to-day again cleaning up billets and surroundings and getting sanitary arrangements made. Received Warning Order for battalion to move forward. Weather dull and threatening rain. Owing to some mistake, an order was circulated to-night ordering the battalion to move immediately. It happened to be an old order, though, which had been mistaken by the Signallers for an order applying to to-day.	

Army Form C. 2118.

WAR DIARY
or
INTELLIGENCE SUMMARY.
(Erase heading not required.)

Instructions regarding War Diaries and Intelligence Summaries are contained in F.S. Regs., Part II. and the Staff Manual respectively. Title pages will be prepared in manuscript.

Place	Date	Hour	Summary of Events and Information	Remarks and references to Appendices
THUN ST.MARTIN.	20.10.18.		Battalion moved from THUN ST.MARTIN to LIEU ST.AMAND by march route leaving Starting point at 07.20. Surplus personnel left at THUN ST.MARTIN, Transport at IWUY. Weather rainy and dull. Surplus personnel moved into Chateau.	OO 219
LIEU ST.AMAND.	21.10.18.		Battalion moved up from LIEU ST.AMAND to NOYELLES, and surplus personnel and Transport moved up to LIEU ST.AMAND. Weather dull & threatening rain.	OO 2/8.
NOYELLES.	22.10.18.		The Battalion lay at NOYELLES.	OO.220
	23.10.18.		The Battalion lay at NOYELLES.	
	24.10.18.		On this morning the crossing of the ECAILLON River was forced by the 153rd Inf.Bde. and in the evening the 152 Inf.Bde. relieved them in the front line. The battalion left billets at 5.30 pm. and moved to a point E. of the GRAND BOIS. at 21.00 hours, guides from the Front Line Coy of the Black Watch conducted "D" Coy 6/7th Gordon Highrs. to the front line positions in and about the SUNKEN ROAD, 500 - 1200 yards SSE. of MAING; the remaining Companies, "C", "B" & "A", following and finding their own way to SUPPORT and RESERVE positions. These were: Old enemy Reserve :- The Sunken Road running NE. from MONCHAUX in J.28. pits and the lanes about 1,000 yards behind (West of) of the front line. Until arrival of orders, Battalion HQ. remained at the W. end of GRAND BOIS. The B.G.C. held a conference here with Battalion C.O's between 23.00 and 24.00 hours, when orders for attack were issued. Battalion HQ. then moved forward to a house on E. bank of ECAILLON River, half-way between MONCHAUX and THIANT.	

Army Form C. 2118.

WAR DIARY
or
INTELLIGENCE SUMMARY.
(Erase heading not required.)

Instructions regarding War Diaries and Intelligence Summaries are contained in F. S. Regs., Part II. and the Staff Manual respectively. Title pages will be prepared in manuscript.

Place	Date	Hour	Summary of Events and Information	Remarks and references to Appendices

MAING.	25.10.18.		During the early hours of this day, Battalion orders for the attack were issued to Company Commanders. "C" Coy was moved up from its Support position to front line on left of "D" Coy, which in to the Right to make room for it. Before midnight, "A" and "B" Coys moved up to positions abut the Hollow and Lane in F.30.a & c. 6th Seaforths on the left of the battalion; 4th Division on the Right.
			
			Attack: Normal formation in two double waves, each Company on a Two Platoon frontage. Dispositions: Left. Right.
			                                                    "C" "D"
			                                                    "B" "A"
			
			Objectives:
			  1st Objective: Line of rifle pits 700 to 800 yards from Jumping-off line.
			  2nd Objective: Railway Embankment in F.20.a & d.
			  3rd Objective: High ground E. of Railway (CAUMONT Farm, OLD REDOUBT and W. edge of ROUGE MONT.)
			
			ZERO hour was 07.00 and the attack was carried out under a creeping barrage. The leading wave went straight on to 2nd Objective which they captured. The 2nd wave mopped-up and remained on the 1st Objective "A" and "B" Coys went through "C" and "D" Coys and captured the final objective. During the day, the two platoons of "C" and "D" Coys were withdrawn from the Railway to line of 1st Objective, where the remainder of these Companies had stayed. About dusk, after a heavy bombardment, the enemy pushed a counter-attack against our front line positions, and our groups holding it were driven back to the Railway Embankment. Battalion H. moved forward to MAING during the day.	

WAR DIARY
or
INTELLIGENCE SUMMARY.

(Erase heading not required.)

Army Form C. 2118.

Place	Date	Hour	Summary of Events and Information	Remarks and references to Appendices
MAING.	26.10.18.		During the night 25th/26th, orders for renewal of the attack were received. 1/4th Gordon Highrs. of the 154 Bde. relieved the 1/6th Seaforths on our Left; a Battalion of the ESSEX Regt. (4th Divn) on our Right. Before daylight, "C" and "D" Coys were moved up to the Railway Embankment. Dispositions for Attack: Left "B" "C" "D" "A" Right.	
			Objectives.	
			First : The High ground on a line through BETERAVE Farm and 100 yards E. of the ROUGE MONT.	
			Second : From the Sunken Road in F.15.b & d. to the road running NE. from FAMARS and 100 yards beyond that village.	Shato vnew K.14.b.4.d.
			ZERO hour: 10.00 hours.	
			The troops went forward behind a creeping barrage; "C" and "D" Coys "leap-frogging" "A" & "B" which captured 1st objective and pushing on to 2nd objective which the<s>y</s> captured and consolidated. The positions captured were consolidated and maintained all day. Half Section of M.G. Coy was pushed forward to pits in F.15.c.	
			Weather was bright and fine, and enemy artillery played on any groups showing themselves for a minute about line of 1st objective or beyond it. The captured positions were heavily shelled from time to time throughout the day. A particularly heavy bombardment towards dusk was followed by a counter-attack which drove some elements of the Battalion on our left back. Our front line, however, held fast and the situation on our left was re-established. At night the dispositions were as follows :— Front Line : Final objective held by half of "D" and half of "C" Coys, with the other half Coys and combined Coy Hqrs. in the Sunken Road running SE. from FAMARS through K.15.a, b & d.; "A" and "B" Coys along the line in front of MONT ROUGE and BETERAVE Farm. After dark, these two Coys were relieved by a Coy of the 7th A & S.Highrs., & moved back to a position in Reserve SE. of MAING in the Sunken Road in J.24.d. and 30.b. **Communication :** The Battalion signallers, as soon as the 1st Objective had been captured, established Visual Signal Stations at the Old Redoubt and the Sunken Road where "A" & "B" Coys were subsequently withdrawn <s>from</s>. For want of cable, messages came by runner from this Station to Battn. HQ. On 27th a cable was laid connecting the Station	

Army Form C. 2118.

WAR DIARY
of
INTELLIGENCE SUMMARY.
(Erase heading not required.)

Instructions regarding War Diaries and Intelligence Summaries are contained in F.S. Regs., Part II. and the Staff Manual respectively. Title pages will be prepared in manuscript.

Place	Date	Hour	Summary of Events and Information	Remarks and references to Appendices
MAING.	26.10.18.		contd. Station with Battalion Hqrs.) The Signal Service was carried on out by night and day and was invaluable.	
	27.10.18.		The relief of the two forward Coys of the battalion was to have been effected by the 4th Gordon Highrs. but the relieving Company became casualties from Gas, and our "C" & "D" Coys were not relieved and remained in front line throughout the day. Enemy artillery bombarded FAMARS & our positions heavily and, during the afternoon, an enemy counter-attack on our left succeded in pushing back the troops on our left and entering the village of FAMARS. Our front line Coys refused their left flank, covered the exits from the village with Lewis Guns and held fast until a counter-attack by the battalion on our left had restored the position and re-established the line. After dark, these two Companies ("C" & "D") were relieved by the 5th Seaforth Highrs. and came back to the Sunken Road where "A" & "B" Coys already were. The Signal Post at the Old Redoubt was relieved by the 5th Seaforths. The Post at Sunken Road was maintained until night of 28th.	
	28.10.18.		The Battalion remained in the Sunken Road SE. of M.ING until the afternoon. At 17.00 hours it was relieved by the 6th Battn. West Yorkshire Regt. and marched back to billets in NEUVILLE-sur-L'ESCAUT.	
NEUVILLE-sur-L'ESCAUT.	29.10.18.		The Battalion lay at NEUVILLE-sur-L'ESCAUT.	OO. 224
THUN LEVEQUE	30.10.18.		The Brigade moved to THUN ST.MARTIN and THUN LEVEQUE; the battalion went into billets in the latter village.	
	31.10.18.		Battalion resting at THUN LEVEQUE.	

J. ~~~~~~ for Lieut.Colonel
Comdg. 1/7 Battalion The Gordon Highrs.

Army Form C. 2118.

WAR DIARY
or
INTELLIGENCE SUMMARY.
(Erase heading not required.)

Instructions regarding War Diaries and Intelligence
Summaries are contained in F. S. Regs., Part II.
and the Staff Manual respectively. Title pages
will be prepared in manuscript.

Place	Date	Hour	Summary of Events and Information	Remarks and references to Appendices
THUN LEVEQUE	31.10.18.			
			HONOURS during month:	
			MILITARY CROSS — Lieutenant T. D. THOMSON.	
			Military Medals — 17. other ranks.	
			Bar to M.M. — 1. other rank.	
			Officers Other Ranks.	
			STRENGTH last month 39 949	
			Increase — 21 434	
			60 1383	
			Decrease — 18 653	
			STRENGTH at the end of this month. 42 730	
			31st October 1918. J. Grant Major Lieut-Colonel,	
			Commanding 6/7th Battalion, The Gordon Highlanders.	

"A"

"Recovered in Front Line during early part of battle 14/15th October 1918."

'A'

51 (H) Div. Signal School.   SS 36.

O.C,
1/6 Gordon Highrs.

No 42226 Pte Gillies. A.
has lost his Tamoshanter.

I shall be glad if he
can be furnished with
one from the Q.M Stores.

[signature]

2nd Lieut.
Commandant.
11/10/1918   51 (H) Div Signal School

"C"

"A" Form
MESSAGES AND SIGNALS.

Army Form C. 2121 (in pads of 100.)

Prefix...... Code ......m.	Words.	Charge.	This message is on a/c of:	Recd. at ......m
Office of Origin and Service Instructions.	Sent		..............Service.	Date ....
....	At......m.			From ....
....	To........			
....	By........		(Signature of "Franking Officer.")	By ....

TO { Headquarters. 152nd Infantry Bde.

Sender's Number.	Day of Month.	In reply to Number.	
OK 150	7/11	E 23/43	AAA

OFFICERS

Lieut (A/Captain) K. Murray   Wounded 25/10/18
Lieutenant A. Riddell   "   "
2nd Lieutenant D.R.A. Walker   "   "
  "   "   R.S. Donald   "   "
  "   "   G. McK. Collier "   "
  "   "   G.W. Conlon   26/10/18

OTHER RANKS.
  Killed   7
  Wounded 104
  MISSING   NIL

From Comdg Gordon Highrs
Place
Time
The above may be forwarded as now corrected. (Z)   Lt. Colonel.
                                Censor.   Signature of Addressor or person authorised to telegraph in his name

6/7th Battalion, The Gordon Highlanders.

NARRATIVE OF OPERATIONS - 11th - 30th October 1918.

BOURLON.
October 11th.
The Battalion left BOURLON by march route to relieve the 21st Canadian Infantry Battalion, 4th Brigade, at 12.30 hours, and passed Starting Point at 13.00. Considerable delay was experienced on the march, especially at CAMBRAI, by the tremendous traffic on the roads.
The Battalion arrived at ESCAUDOEVRES at 17.00.
At 19.15 the Battalion moved forward to take over the front line Colonel THOM went on in advance of the Battalion, and Major CRAN & Lieut. COLLIER brought on Battalion, and at 02.30 the Front Line relief was commenced and by 03.30 the relief was completed. Echelon "B" established at T.20d.

IWUY,
AVESNES-LE-SEC. **October 12th.**
Battalion went into position along road at 03.30 and at 12.00 went into action with objective along the road from 0.8.c.8.3 to 0.15.c.9.3; the advance was met by little opposition, and with only about 30 casualties of which mostly all were slight, and objective was reached by 14.00, and our main line of resistance was established at Sunken Road in front of MILL, and here the Companies dug themselves in; the Support Companies dug-in on Road at rear of MILL; Battalion H.Qrs. were established at the Mill (MOULIN de PIERRE).

October 13th.
After artillery had bombarded enemy positions, the Battalion at 09.00 attacked with objectives : The wood and railway directly in front. Severe opposition was met by M.G. fire from wood and railway. At 10.30 the battalion retired back to its original jumping-off position of this morning; this retirement proved a very difficult matter and was only completed at 12.00.
At 08.30 Colonel THOM was wounded in the leg whilst taking observations from the top of the Mill (MOULIN de PIERRE). Major CRAN and Captain RISK (who had just reported in off leave yesterday) were ordered up and to be prepared to go into action. Colonel LAURIE of the Seaforths was put in command of all the Battalions in the front line. During the day the Battalion suffered heavy casualties, Lieut. HENDERSON being killed and 7 other Officers wounded, Captain A. Reid severely; 22 men were killed, 271 wounded & gassed and 17 men missing, 4 men died of wounds.

October 14th.
Our artillery heavily bombarded the Wood and Railway from 08.00 until 09.00 and also again from 09.30 until 10.00, after which we sent out a patrol of 20 men under Sergeant STABLES to reconnoitre Wood, and at the same time the Seaforths sent out patrol to reconnoitre Railway with the object in both cases of obtaining information as regards enemy strength at these two particular spots where the attack had been held up yesterday. At 11.30 word was brought back by one of our patrol to the effect that they had found the enemy in great strength, in machine guns especially in the one corner of the Wood and at a house at the point where the road crosses the railway. Patrol reported as unable to get back until night owing to enemy alertness, and they were taking cover at about point 0.9.c.7.3. The man who brought this information was a volunteer from the patrol. However, at 16.30 Sergt. STABLES reported at Battalion H.Qrs. to the effect that the Patrol had got back, but had 2 men killed and 3 wounded; he had managed to get the wounded in. This N.C.O. gave an excellent report of his patrol's work, and the information obtained was of the greatest value, and enabled the artillery to get to work at 17.30 on the Wood and Railway. At 19.00 the Battalion was relieved from the front line by the 6th Seaforths. (contd-

2nd Sheet.

IWUY,
AVESNES-LE-SEC.
(contd.)

October 14th contd.
During the early part of the evening the enemy put over a good deal of BLUE CROSS and YELLOW CROSS Gas. Captain REID reported as having died of wounds, received here yesterday. The battalion moved back to Sunken Road at 00.31 and men settled down in Cubby-holes after receiving a good hot meal. During the night the enemy heavily shelled this area with BLUE and YELLOW CROSS Gas.

October 15th.
Battalion in Reserve in SUNKEN ROAD, O.31. c & d. Enemy heavily shelled area during the day and night.
"D" Company taken into IWUY and billeted there.
All Coys had Baths at "D" Coy's new Billets at IWUY.

October 16th.
Battalion still in SUNKEN ROAD, situated as described yesterday.
One of our "B" Coy's men, who had been wounded on the 14th near the Wood, managed to crawl back and confirmed the information Sergt. STABLES patrol had brought back.

October 17th.
The battalion lay in the same positions, 3 Coys in the SUNKEN ROAD and "D" Coy in IWUY.
Lt-Col.C.J.E.CRANSTOUN rejoined from leave and assumed command.
The 152nd Bde. was relieved by the 154 Bde. The 1/4th Seaforth Highrs. relieved the 6/7th Gordon Highrs. during the afternoon, and on ~~the afternoon~~ relief the Battalion marched back to billets in THUN ST.MARTIN.

October 18. and 19th.
The battalion lay at THUN ST.MARTIN.

October 20th.
Orders for the forward move of the 152nd Inf.Bde. were received on the 19th and were carried out on this day.
The 6/7th Gordon Highrs. moved at 07.35 and marched by IWUY and HORDAIN to LIEU ST.AMAND, reaching it at 10.30. Weather dark and wet. Dinners were taken at 11.30 in readiness for a further move, which however did not take place, and the Battalion settled in for the night.

October 21st.
At 11.00 the 152nd Inf.Bde. moved to NOYELLES and DOUCHY. The 6/7th Gordon Highrs. to NOYELLES, where they went into billets soon after midday.

October 22 and 23rd.
The battalion lay at NOYELLES

October 24th. (Map Ref.- 51A., 1/40,000.).
On this morning, the crossing of the ECAILLON River was forced by the 153rd Bde. and in the evening the 152 Bde. relieved them in front line.
The battalion left Billets at 5.30 pm. and moved to a point E. of the GRAND BOIS.
At 9 p.m. guides from the Front Line Coy of the 6th Black Watch conducted "D" Coy, 6/7th Gordon Highrs. to the front line positions in and about the Sunken Road, 500 to 1200 yds SSE. of MAING; the remaining Coys, C, B & A, following & finding their own way to SUPPORT and RESERVE positions.
These were - Support : Old enemy pits and the lanes about 1,000 yards behind (West of) the front line.
Reserve : The Sunken Road running NE. from MONCHAUX in J.28.
Until arrival of orders, Battn.HQ. remained at the W. end of GRAND BOIS.
The B.G.C. held a conference here with Battn. C.O's between 23.00 and 24.00, when orders for attack were issued. Battn.HQ. then moved forward to a house on E. bank of ECAILLON River, half-way between MONCHAUX and THIANT.

3rd Sheet.

October 25th.
During the early hours of this day, Battalion Orders for the attack were issued to Company Commanders.
"C" Coy was moved up from its Support position to front line on left of "D" Coy, which closed in to the right to make room for it.
Before daylight, "A" and "B" Coys moved up to positions about the Hollow and Lane in J.30 a & c.
6th Seaforths on the left of the Battalion.
4th Division on the Right " " "

Attack: Normal formation in two double waves; each Company on a two Platoon frontage.

Dispositions:
LEFT.	RIGHT.
"C"	"D"
"B"	"A".

Objectives:
  1st Objective: Line of rifle pits 700 to 800 yards from Jumping-off line.
  2nd Objective: Railway embankment in K.20.a & d.
  3rd Objective: High ground E. of Railway (CAUMONT FARM, OLD REDOUBT and W. edge of ROUGE MONT).

ZERO hour was 07.00 and attack was carried out under a creeping barrage. The leading wave went straight on to 2nd Objective which they captured. The 2nd wave mopped-up and remained on the 1st Objective. "A" and "B" Coys went through "C" and "D" Coys and captured the final objective.
During the day the two platoons of "C" and "D" Coys were withdrawn from the railway to line of first objective, where the remainder of these Coys had stayed.
About dusk, after a heavy bombardment, the enemy pushed a counter-attack against our front line positions, and our groups holding it were driven back to the Railway Embankment.
Battn.H.Qrs. moved forward to MAING during the day.

October 26th.
During the night 25th/26th, orders for renewal of the attack were received.
1/4th Gordon Highrs. of 154 Bde. relieved the 1/6th Seaforths on our Left; a battalion of the ESSEX REGT.(4th Divn.) on our Right.
Before daylight, "C" and "D" Coys were moved up to the Railway Embankment.

Dispositions for attack:
LEFT.	RIGHT.
"B"	"A"
"C"	"D".

Objectives:
  First: the high ground on a line through BETERAVE Farm and 100 yards E. of the ROUGE MONT.
  Second: from the Sunken Road in K.15.b & d. to the road running NE. from FAMARS and 100 yards beyond that village.

ZERO hour - 10.00 hours.
The troops went forward behind a creeping barrage; "C" & "D" Coys "leap-frogging" "A" & "B" which captured 1st Objective and pushing on to 2nd Objective, which they captured and consolidated. The positions captured were consolidated and maintained all day.
Half Section of the M.G.Coy was pushed forward to pits in K.15.c.
Weather was bright & fine, and enemy artillery played on any groups showing themselves for a minute about line of 1st Objective or beyond it. The captured positions were heavily shelled from time to time throughout the day.
A particularly heavy bombardment towards dusk was followed by a counter-attack which drove some elements of the Battalion on our left back. Our front line, however, held fast and the situation on our left was re-established.
                                        (contd.

4th Sheet.

October 26th.   contd.
At night, the dispositions were as follows :-
Front Line :   Final Objective held by half of "D" and half of "C" Coys, with the other half Coys and combined Coy HQ. in the Sunken Road running SE. from FAMARS through K.15.a,b & d.; "A" and "B" Coys along the line in front of MONT ROUGE and BETERAVE Farm.
   After dark, these two Coys were relieved by a Coy of the 7th A & S.Highrs., and moved back to a position in Reserve SE. of MAING in the Sunken Road in J.24.d. and 30.b.
Communication : The Battalion Signallers, as soon as the first objective had been captured, established Visual Signal Stations at the OLD REDOUBT and the Sunken Road where "A" and "B" Coys were subsequently withdrawn to. For want of cable, messages came by runner from this station to Battn.HQ. (On 27th a cable was laid connecting the Station with Battn.Hqrs.)
   The Signal Service was carried on by night and day and was invaluable.

October 27th.
   The relief of the two forward Coys of the Battalion was to have been effected by the 4th Gordon Highrs., but the relieving Company became casualties from Gas, and our "C" and "D" Coys were not relieved, and remained in front line throughout the day.
   Enemy artillery bombarded FAMARS and our positions heavily and, during the afternoon, an enemy counter-attack on our left succeeded in pushing back the troops on our left and entering the village of FAMARS.   Our front line Coys refused their left flank, covered the exits from the village with Lewis Guns and held fast until a counter-attack by the battalion on our left had restored the position and re-established the line.
   After dark, these two Coys ("C" and "D") were relived by the 5th Seaforth Highrs. and came back to the Sunken Road, where "A" and "B" Coys already were.
   The Signal Post at the OLD REDOUBT was relieved by the 5th Seaforths.
   The Post at Sunken Road was maintained by 6/7th Gordon Highrs. until night of 28th.

October 28th.
   The Battalion remained in the Sunken Road SE. of MAING until the afternoon.   At 17.00 hours it was relieved by the 6th Battn West Yorkshire Regt. and marched back to billets in NEUVILLE-sur-L'ESCAUT.

October 29th.
   The Battalion lay at NEUVILLE-sur-L'ESCAUT.

October 30.
   The Brigade moved to THUN ST.MARTIN and THUN LEVEQUE.
The battalion went into billets in the latter village.

2nd Nov. 1918.   C.E.Cranston   Lieut-Colonel,
                              Comdg 6/7th Bn., The Gordon Highlanders.

Casualties. *War Diary.*

"B"

Headquarters,
152nd Infantry Brigade.

Herewith corrected Casualty Return in accordance with your wire S.R.324 dated 17.10.18.

(1) 10/11th October to 23.59 14th Oct.1918.

Officers:
    Lt-Col.J.G.Thom, DSO,MC.   — Wounded   13.10.18.
    2/Lt.R.I.Frans (Cameron Highrs) "   "
    A/Captain A.Reid   — Died of Wds. "
    2/Lieut.G.G.Hastings   — Wounded   "
    "   E.C.Macdonald   — "   "
    Lieut.R.J.Henderson   — Killed   "
    2/Lieut.F.Hall   — Wounded   "
    Lieut.J.B.Paterson   — "   "

Other Ranks:
    Killed   —   22.
    Wounded   —   271.
    Missing   —   17.
    Died of Wds. —   4.
                 314

(ii) 00.01 15th Oct.1918 to date.

Officers: Nil.

Other Ranks:
    Killed   —   1.
    Wounded   —   14.
    Missing   —   Nil.

19th October 1918.   C.E. Cranston
                                             Lieut-Colonel,
                                         Comdg 6/7th Bn., The Gordon Highlanders.

Operation Order No. 212

2nd October, 1918.

Reference Maps:-
    CAMBRAI 51B - 1/10,000.
    51B.N.W. - 1/20,000.

1. RELIEF:
    The 6th Bn., The Gordon Highlanders will be relieved to-day by the 2nd Devon Regiment.
    Orders as to the relief of Companies and providing of guides will be issued later.

2. MOVE:
    After relief, the Battalion will move by 'busses to the FLAVIN CAPELLE Area; Battalion Headquarters, the Mairie, FLAVIN CAPELLE.
        Embussing point - AYETTE CROSS ROADS K.14.b.35..5.
        Time   - 16.00 hours.
    Lieut. J. McKAY and 1 N.C.O. of "A" Coy. will be at Embussing point at 15.00 hours and will have lorries marked off by Companies. Lewis Guns and Magazines will be taken in the lorries.

3. ADVANCE PARTY:
    Lieut. J.J. ROY and 1 N.C.O. per Company and 1 for Headquarters will report to Brigade Transport Officer at ELLISBURGH DUMP at 00.00 hours to-day. The party will be conveyed by lorry to FLAVIN CAPELLE and will report to the Area Commandant there for accommodation.

4. PERSONNEL LEFT AT TRANSPORT LINES:
    Party will move to FLAVIN CAPELLE Area by march route to-day under orders to be issued by Lieut. A. GRAY.

5. BATTN. TRANSPORT:
    Transport (less Cookers and Mess Cart) will move under orders to be issued by Brigade Transport Officer.

6. DEFENCE SCHEMES:
    All Defence Schemes, Maps 1/10,000 and 1/20,000, Air Photographs and 153rd Infantry Brigade Order No. 339 with map attached - "Action in case of Hostile Withdrawal" will be handed over, and receipts sent to Battalion Headquarters within one hour of handing over.

7. COMPLETION OF RELIEF:
    Completion of relief will be notified to Battalion Headquarters by the code word "TORPEY".

8. ARRIVAL IN BILLETS:
    Companies settled in billets will be reported to Battalion Headquarters.

9. ACKNOWLEDGE.

                    sd/. J. GILLIES, Lieut. & A/Adjutant,
                         6th Bn., The Gordon Highlanders.

Issued at 9.30 a.m. 2.10.18.

Copies to :- 1   File.
              2   H.Q., 153rd Inf. Bde.
              3   O.C., 2nd Devon Regt.
          4 - 7   Coy. Miss.
              8   H.Q. Details.
              9   H.Q. Mess.
             10   M.O.
             11   T.O.
             12   War Diary.

SECRET.   THE GORDON HIGHLANDERS.   Copy No. ......

ADMINISTRATIVE INSTRUCTIONS ISSUED IN CONJUNCTION WITH O.O. No. 212.
_____

                              2nd October, 1918.
                              _____

1. TRENCH STORES:
    Trench Stores will be handed over to Advance Party, 2nd Devon
Regiment and receipts forwarded to Battalion Headquarters before
embussing.
    Certificates will be obtained as to cleanliness of billets and
areas and forwarded at the same time.
    Transport Officer will obtain and forward at first opportunity
a certificate of cleanliness for the Horse Lines.

2. WATER TINS:
    Transport Officer will draw any tins required to make up Water
Cart Establishment from Corporal BURNETT, Brigade Headquarters S.A.
Store.
    The 6 extra pack saddles will be retained.

3. MESS TINS:
    Transport Officer will detail transport to collect Officers'
Mess Tins, Orderly Room Boxes, etc., at 14.00 hours. When loaded
this section with Company Cookers will move under an N.C.O. to be
detailed by the Transport Officer.

4. S.A.A. STORES:
    One lorry will be at BRIGADE HEADQUARTERS at 08.00 hours to-day
to move Stores.

                              sd/ J. GRIFFIN, Lieut: & O/Adjutant,
                                    6th Bn., The Gordon Highlanders.

    Copies to all regiments of I.... Bde. 212.

SECRET.   THE GORDON HIGHLANDERS.   Copy No...11...

Operation Order No. 213.

5th October, 1918.

Reference Maps :-
    Sheet 51c. (1/40,000).
    L'Ms 11 (1/100,000).

1.   The Battalion Transport will move to-morrow 6th instant to Canadian Corps Area D.
        Exact location of new Transport lines will be notified later.

2.   Starting Point   -   Cross Roads, F.15.d.6.0.

        Time at Starting Point - 09.55 hours.

        Route   -   ARRAS - GUEMAPPE - CHERISY - HENDECOURT
                             - CAGNICOURT.

3.   During the move, Transport will move forward in groups of not more than four wagons at 300 yards interval. Tracks are to be used where available. In order to avoid the appearance of a column on the march, it is most essential that these intervals are strictly preserved during all halts.

4.   Owing to length of march, Transport will not be overloaded.

5.   Transport will continue the march by day on 7th October to take over from a Battalion of the 9th Canadian Infantry Brigade under orders to be issued later.

6.   ATTACHMENTS.

                                sd/ J. COUTTS, Lieut. & A/Adjutant,
                                    6th Bn., The Gordon Highlanders.

Issued at 20.00 hours, 5/10/18.

Copies to -

        No. 1. File.
            2. H.Q., 152nd Inf. Bde.
         3 - 6. Companies.
            7. T.O.
            8. Q.M.
            9. O. I/c H.Q. Details.
           10. H.Q. Mess.
           11. War Diary.

SECRET. THE GORDON HIGHLANDERS. Copy No......

Operation Order No. 215.

11th October, 1918.

1. The line reached last evening by the Canadian Corps runs through U.S.central, S. and W. of IWUY to N.34.central. The area between the SENSEE and the CANAL de L'ESCAULT is reported clear of the enemy.

2. The Canadian Corps is continuing the advance to-day with its right flank on the CAMBRAI - SAULZOIR Road.
    The 49th Division is on the right, and the 2nd Canadian Div. on the left of the Canadian Corps Front.
    The dividing line between these two Divisions runs from IWUY STATION (T.6.c.) along the IWUY - AVESNES -LE-SEC Road through O.32.a. (inclusive 2nd Can. Div.) and thence to O.12.central.
    The line to be reached to-day runs from SAULZOIR (E.26.d.) through AVESNES-LE-SEC to LIEU - ST. AMAND.
    As soon as the 2nd Can. Div. has cleared IWUY, the 11th Div. is to pass a Brigade across the CANAL de L'ESCAULT and clear the area between the IWUY - BOUCHAIN Road and the CANAL de L'ESCAULT, extending the left flank of the 2nd Can. Div.

3. The Brigade will move to IWUY and THUN -ST. MARTIN, 6/7th Gordon Hs. leading.
    Brigade Starting Point - Cross Roads at F.3.d.4.1.
    Time to pass Starting Point - Zero plus 30.
    Route - Cross Roads at F.3.d.4.1. - Track through F.4.c. and d.
            - Cross Roads at A.9.a.4.1. - S.24.c.3.4. - ESCADOEUFRES
            - IWUY.
    Dress - Fighting Order.
    Distances - 100 yards between Companies.
                100 yards between Transport and rear Company.
                50 yards between sections of 12 vehicles.

4. Failing further orders the Battalion will halt when the head of the column reaches Road Junction, S.24.c.3.4. Battalion will then close up, Transport will pass clear of the Road whenever possible and men will have dinner.

5. Quartermaster will detail a guide to be at Cross Roads X.28.central RAILLENCOURT at 13.00 hours to-day to guide Supply Wagons to Battln.

6. ACKNOWLEDGE.

Lieut. & A/Adjutant,
6/7th Bn., The Gordon Highlanders.

SECRET.

W.D

THE GORDON HIGHLANDERS.

Copy No........

Operation Order No. 215.

10th October, 1918.

Reference Map :-
   Sheet 57C 1/40,000.

1. MOVE.
   The 152nd Infantry Brigade will move on 10th October 1918, by march route from D Reserve Area to B Sub Area (immediately East of BOURLON WOOD) to take the place of 9th Canadian Infantry Brigade.

2. MARCH.
   The Battalion will form up at 11.15 hours in column of route on RIENCOURT - QUEANT Road facing South East with the head of the column at D Coy's Dugouts in the following order - H.Q., D, A, B, C.
   Brigade Starting Point - QUEANT Cross Roads, D.2.c.0.0.
   Battalion's Time to pass Starting Point -
      5th Bn. The Seaforth Highrs. - 11.00 hours.
      6th   "   "   "   "   - 11.15   "
      6/7th "   " Gordon   "   - 11.30   "

   Route - QUEANT - PRONVILLE - Tracks running from PRONVILLE - INCHY Road at D.4.a.4.4. to D.10.d. to D.11.c. to D.17.b. to E.13. to MOEUVRES, thence to BAPAUME - CAMBRAI Road at E.28.c.0.2. - ANNEUX Chapel
   Distance - 200 yards between Companies.

3. ADVANCE PARTY.
   Party as already detailed will report to Staff Captain at E.12.c.0.7. at 10.00 hours.

4. TRANSPORT.
   Transport will move separately as under :-
   Brigade Starting Point and Route - (As for Battalion).
   6/7th Bn. The Gordon Highlanders (leading) pass Starting Point at 12.05 hours.
   100 yards between Transport of Units.
   Strict march discipline will be enforced in the move. Drivers will carry whips and brakesmen will not place rifles or packs on vehicles.

5. AREAS.
   Areas vacated will be left thoroughly clean and a certificate to this effect will be rendered to Orderly Room before moving off.

6.   Arrival in New Area to be reported at once to Battalion Hdqrs.

7.   ACKNOWLEDGE.

                                                    [signature]
                                        Lieut. & A/Adj.,
                                6/7th Bn., The Gordon Highlanders.

Issued at 08.50 hours, 10.10.18.

Copies to -
        No. 1   File.
           2   H.Q., 152nd Inf. Bde.
        3 - 6   Companies.
           7   O. i/c H.Q. Details.
           8   M.O.
           9   T.O.
          10   H.Q. Mess.
          11   War Diary.

SECRET.   THE GORDON HIGHLANDERS.   Copy No........

ADMINISTRATIVE INSTRUCTIONS issued in conjunction with O.O. No. 215.

10th October, 1918.

1.   Balmorals will be worn on the march.

2.   A motor lorry is allotted to the Battalion to move baggage and may be used for two journeys.
     Transport Officer will send Battalion Transport a second journey if necessary.

3.   Q.M. Stores are in F.12.d. and F.18.b.

4.   Transport Lines will be allotted to the Battalion by Lieut. ROBERTSON.

5.   There are Water Cart Refilling points in BOURLON VILLAGE.

6.   Officers' Valises, Mess Kits, will be dumped on Road beside Orderly Room at 10.00 hours.

                                           Lieut. & A/Adjutant,
                              6/7th Bn., The Gordon Highlanders.

Copies to all recipients of O.O. No. 215.

SECRET.   THE GORDON HIGHLANDERS.   COPY NO....11..

Operation Order No. 215.

16th October, 1918.

Reference Map :-
    Sheet 57C 1/40,000.

1. MOVE.
    The 152nd Infantry Brigade will move on 16th October 1918, by march route from D Reserve Area to B Sub Area (immediately East of BOURLON WOOD) to take the place of 9th Canadian Infantry Brigade.

2. MARCH.
    The Battalion will form up at 11.15 hours in column of route on RUMILCOURT - QUEANT Road, facing South East with the head of the column at D Coy's Dugouts in the following order - H.Q., D, A, B, C.
    Brigade starting point - QUEANT Cross Roads, D.2.c.d.w.
    Battalion's Time to pass Starting Point:-
        5th Bn. The Seaforth Highrs. - 11.00 hours.
        6th "   "   "   "   - 11.15   "
        6/7th "   "   Gordon   "   - 11.30   "

    Route - QUEANT - PRONVILLE - Tracks running from PRONVILLE -
            INCHY Road at J42.a.4.4. to D.10.d. to D.11.c. to
            D.17.b. to E.13. to MOEUVRES, thence to BAPAUME
            CAMBRAI Road at E.29.a.0.2. - ANNEUX Chapel
    Distance - 200 yards between Companies.

3. ADVANCE PARTY.
    Party as already detailed will report to Staff Captain at E.12.c.w.7. at 10.00 hours.

4. TRANSPORT.
    Transport will move separately as under :-
    Brigade starting point and Route - (as for Battalion).
    6/7th Bn. The Gordon Highlanders (leading) pass starting point at 12.05 hours.
    100 yards between Transport of Units.
    Strict march discipline will be enforced in ~~transport~~ move ~~ment~~. Drivers will carry whips and brakesmen will not place rifles or packs on vehicles.

5. AREAS.
    Areas vacated will be left thoroughly clean and a certificate to this effect will be rendered to Orderly Room before moving off.

6.   Arrival in New Area to be reported at once to Battalion Hdqrs.

7.   A C K N O W L E D G E.

                            sd/ W. CARTIER, Lieut. & A/Adj.,
                                6/7th Bn., The Gordon Highlanders.

Issued at 08.50 hours, 16.10.18.

Copies to -
        No. 1   File.
           2   H.Q. 152nd Inf. Bde.
         3 - 6 Companies.
           7   O. i/c H.Q. Details.
           8   Q.M.
           9   T.O.
          10   H.Q. Mess.
          11   War Diary.

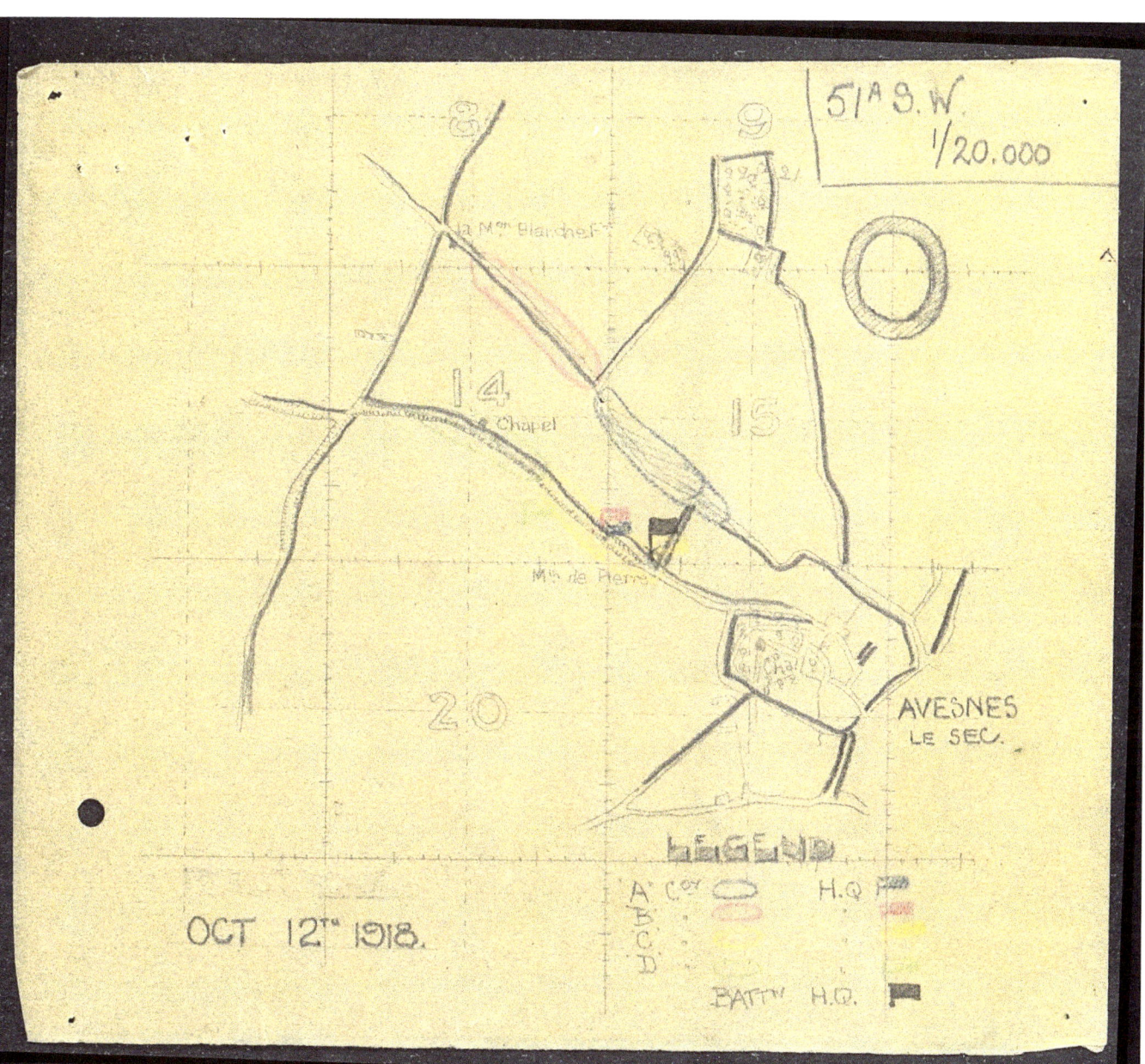

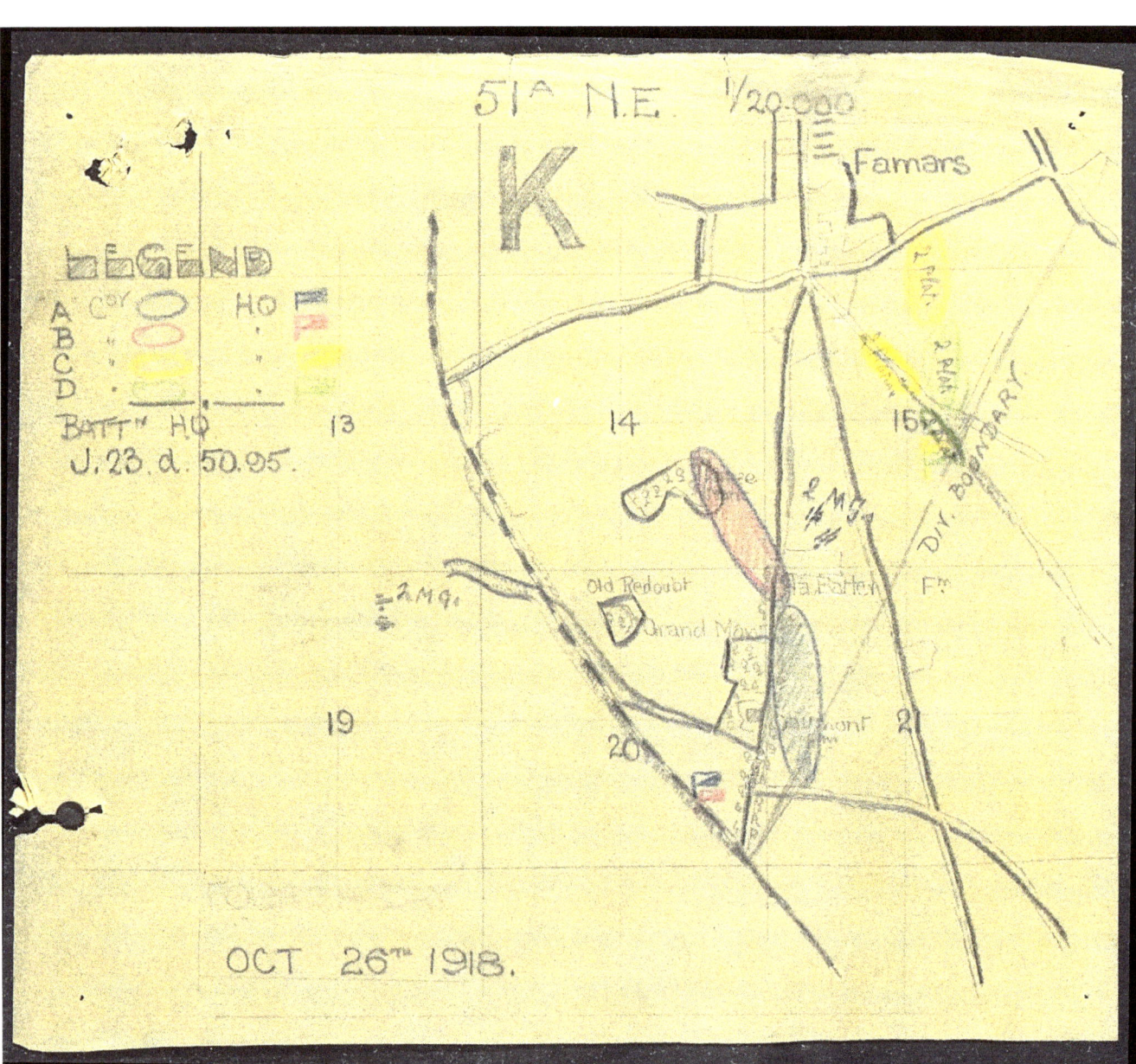

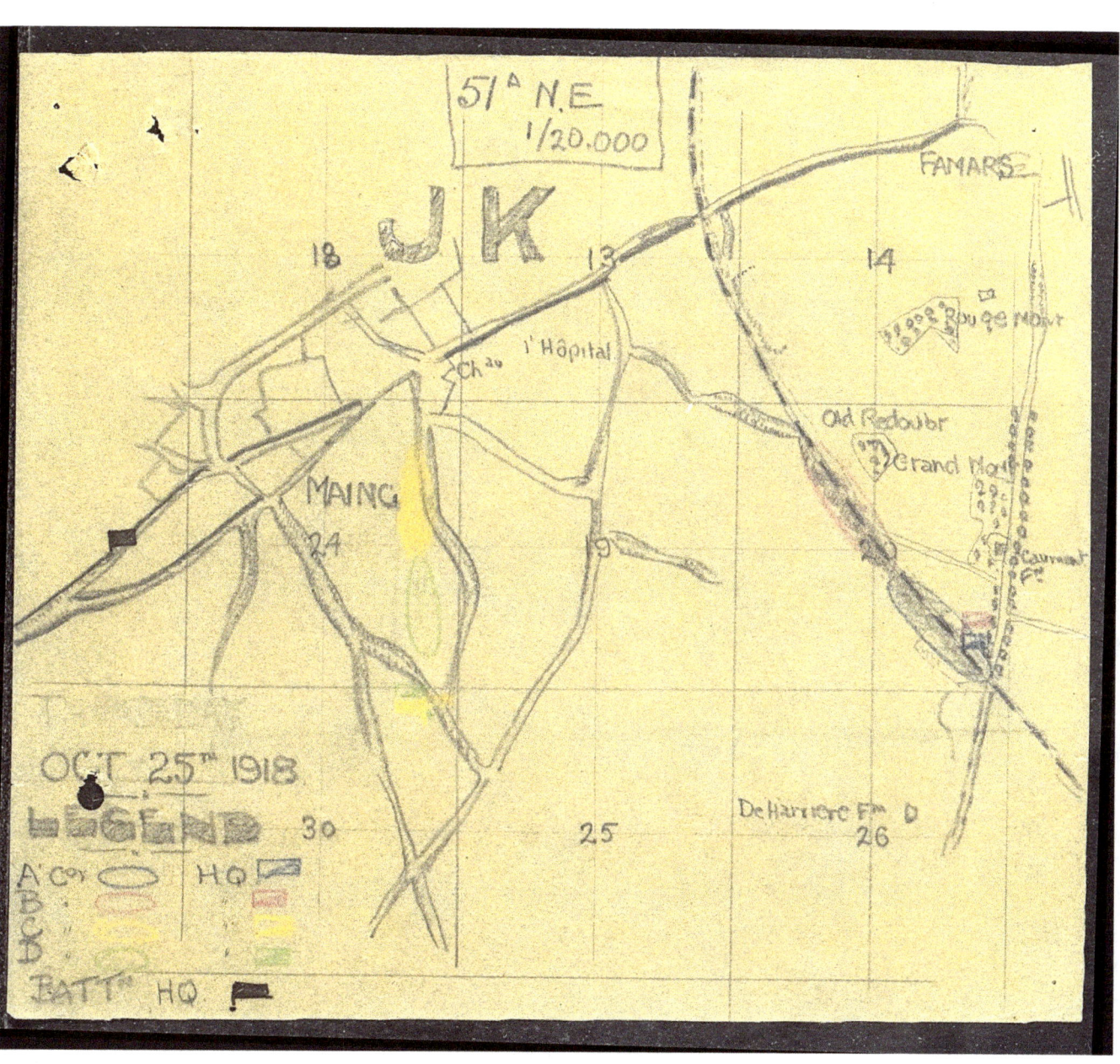

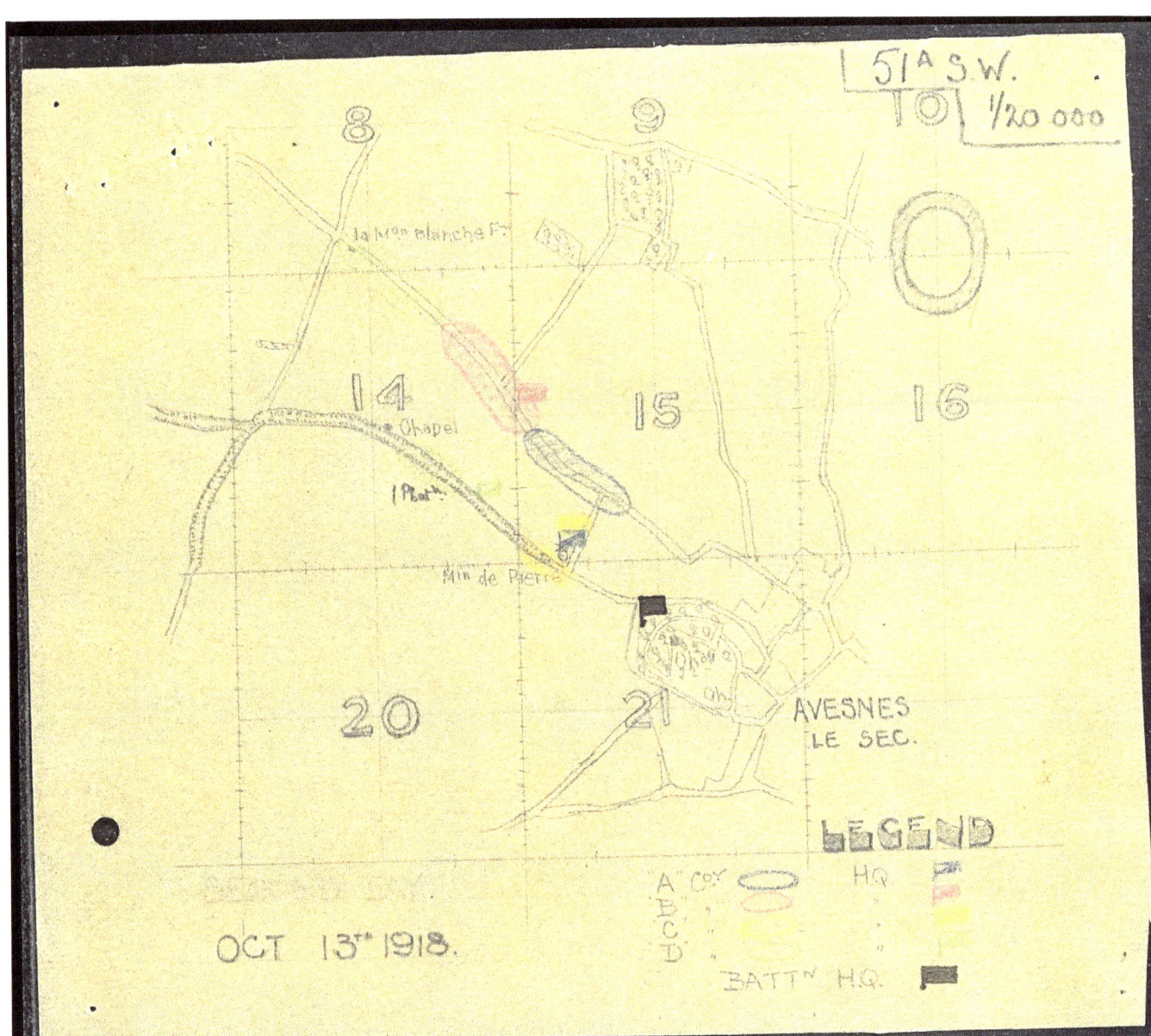

SECRET 6/7th Bn. Gordon Highlanders
OPERATION ORDERS No. 216
4th October, 1918

Ref. Map :- 51A. 1/40,000

1. In continuation of Warning Order X.289, Battn. will be relieved as follows after dusk to-night :-

A, B & C Coys., 6/7th Bn. Gordon Highrs. will be relieved by C Coy. 6th Seaforth Highrs.; D Coy. 6/7th Bn. Gordon Highrs. will be relieved by D Coy. 6th Seaforth Highrs.

2. On relieving Company Commanders taking over, Coys. will proceed at intervals of 200 yards, by parties equivalent to half-platoons, to road at O.31 and O.32. where accommodation is being arranged by Advance Party under Lieut. C. A. COWIE.

3. Guides will be found by 6th Seaforth Highrs. for their own Coys.

4/

- 2 -

4. Cooker Boxes will be left at MILL in charge of Sgt. MAYN who will await arrival of limber which will be sent forward by T.O.

5. Lewis Guns and L.G. magazines etc., will be carried out by Coys.

6. Coys. will report relief complete by Runner.

7. All S.O.S. Rockets will be handed over. O.C. "A" Coy. will hand over 8 Boxes S.A.A. at MILL.

8. Companies will ACKNOWLEDGE

P. Risk
Capt & Adjt.
6/7th Bn. Gordon Highrs

SECRET

W.D/

The Gordon Highlanders
ADMINISTRATIVE INSTRUCTIONS
issued in conjunction with O.O. 217

14th October 1918.

1. Limbers as follows will report at respective HQrs at 14.30 hours –

    1 for Bn. HQ and "C" Coy
    1 " "A" & "B" Coys.
    1 " "D" Coy

    Lewis Guns & L.G. magazines etc. will be loaded on these limbers and taken to new area.

    Blankets at present in possession will be rolled and carried round haversack.

2. Immediately after dinners, cookers will march to new area.

3. Trench Shelters will be handed over to incoming unit and receipts taken.

    These receipts will be forwarded by 18.00 hours on 14th inst.

4. Echelon "B" will move to new area under orders of Capt PATERSON

R Risk
Captain & Adjt;
6/7th Bn. The Gordon Highrs.

Copies to all recipients of O.O. No 214

SECRET.

~~J.L. COY~~

The Gordon Highlanders
OPERATION ORDERS No. 217
17th October, 1918.

Ref. Map:-
Sheet 51A. 1/40.000

1. The 6/7th Bn. Gordon Highlanders will be relieved in reserve to-day by 4th Bn. Seaforth Highlanders, and on relief, will take over area vacated by 4th Seaforth Highrs at T.3.b.47.00.

2. Relief will be carried out as follows:-
Coy. 4th S.H. will take over from Coy 6/7th G.H.
" " " " " " " " "
" " " " " " " " "
" " " " " " " " "

3. Guides from 6/7th Gordon Hs. will rendezvous as follows:-
at N.36.c.9.1 at 14.30 hours.
   2 from Bn. H.Q.
   A, B and C Coys - 1 per Coy. H.Q and 1 per Platoon
at road junction T.5.C.4.9 at 14.30 hours.
   D Coy. - 1 per Coy. H.Q and 1 per Platoon.

4. On relief Battn will proceed as follows to new area -
N.36.d.2.0., Tracks through T.6.a. & C., T.5.d., T.11.b & a., THUN-ST. MARTIN.
   H.Q. and Coys. will each detail a N.C.O. to report to Lieut. J.L. HAY at Bn. H.Q. at 13.00 hours to-day. This party will reconnoitre route laid down and will meet the Battn at N.36.d.2.0.
   H.Q and Coys. will march to new area by parties equivalent to half Platoons in strength and at 100 yards distance.

5. Lieut. J. COLLIER and Advance Party from Echelon B will report at H.Q. 4th Seaforth Highrs at 13.00 hours to take over accommodation.

6/

-2-

6. Completion of relief will be notified to Bn. H.Q. by runner. Arrival in new area will also be reported by runner.

7. ACKNOWLEDGE.

A Risk
Captain,
Adjutant.
6/7th Bn. The Gordon Highrs

Copies to :-
   No. 1   File (Lt COLLIER) ✓
      2   H.Q. 152nd Infy. Brigade
     3-6 Companies
      7   Q.M and T.O.
      8   H.Q. Details
      9   H.Q. Mess.
     10 O.C. 4th Seaforth Highrs

SECRET.   Copy No.

                        The Gordon Highlanders.

    Reference   OPERATION ORDER No. 218.
    Sheet 51A.

1. **Move.**
   The 6/7th Bn., The Gordon Highlanders will move by road to area about LIEU ST. AMAND to-day, Oct. 20.

2. **Orders for the March.**
   Starting point   :   Road Junction T.3.d.6.3.
   Time   :   07.20 hours.
   Route   :   Cross Roads at T.10.a.6.2 - Road Junction
                        T.15.b.5.6, thence main IWUY - HORDAIN Road -
                        Road Junction N.6.a.0.0. - LIEU ST. AMAND.

   Order of March   :   Bn.H.Qrs., A, B, C, D Coys.
                        Limbers, travelling kitchens will march in rear of their respective Coys. Water Carts, Maltese Cart and Mess Cart will march in rear of the battalion.

   Distance   :   100 yards between Companies.

   Dress   :   Fighting Order; greatcoats will be rolled bandolier and tied round the haversack.

3. **Advance Party.**
   Lieutenant J.L. HAY and 2/Lieut. R. HENRY will report at Battalion HQ. at 06.15 to-day to go in advance and reconnoitre the new area.
   Transport Officer will detail horses for these officers.

4. **Echelon "B".**
   Echelon "B" will remain in THUN ST. MARTIN and will be located in the CHATEAU.
   In order to make up the number of Echelon "B", O.C. Companies may include men on leave and courses.
   The following Officers and Warrant Officer will be left out :-
           Major J. Cran,
           Lieut. J. Collier,
   C Coy   265154 C.S.M. J.W. Chalmers, MC, DCM.

5. Battalion Transport and Quartermaster's Stores will move to N.29.c and d. to-day at 08.00 hours.

6. **Acknowledge.**

                                                        [signature]

20th Oct. 1918.
                                                        Captain & Adjutant,
                                                        6/7th Bn., The Gordon Highlanders.

    Distribution :
       Copies 1 - 4.   O.C. Coys.
                  5.   152nd Inf. Bde.
                  6.   O.i/c. Bn. HQ.
                  7.   Transport Officer.
                  8.   Quartermaster.
                  9.   H.Q. Officers' Mess.
                 10.   War Diary.
                 11.   File.

Secret. The Gordon High[rs] Copy No. 11

OPERATION ORDER No. 219.

31st Oct 1918

1. In continuation of Warning Order the Battalion will march to ~~Flesquery~~ NOVELLES to-day as follows:-

   Starting Point : O.1.d.5.5
   Time : 11-20 am
   Route : Track through O.2 and L.33 and 34.
   Order of March : Bn H.Qrs - A - B - C - D Coys
   Transport as yesterday

2. Billets will be left scrupulously clean and a certificate to that effect rendered to Orderly Room.

3. ACKNOWLEDGE

R.R.R.R
Capt & Adjt
6/7th Gordon High[rs]

Distribution:
 Copies 1-4. O.C. Coys.
 5. O/C O/Hd
 6. 152nd Inf Bde
 7. Cpl Thomson
 8. W.D.
 9. File

SECRET.   The Gordon Highlanders.   Copy No. W.D.

Reference Sheet   **OPERATION ORDER No. 220**

MAING
1/20,000   24th Oct. 1918.

1. The battalion will move from NOYELLES to _____ today as follows:—

   Starting Point   :   I. 35. a. 2. 9.
   Time   :   17.10 hours
   Route   :   I. 35. a. 30.25 — MAISON ROUGE — I. 36. b. 6. 5 — track along E. side of railway to J. 15. c. 0. 6.

   Order of March   :   Bn. H.Qrs. "A", "B", "C", "D" Coys.
   ~~Transport will march as before~~
   • Cookers & Coy limbers will march behind their respective Coys. Mess Carts & Water Carts will rejoin Transport.
   Distance   :   100 yds between platoons.

2. Acknowledge.

                                            A. Rush
                                            Capt. & Adjt.
                                            6/7th Gordon Highlanders.

Distribution:
   Copies 1-4. OC Coys
          5.   O/c Hqrs
          6.   152nd Inf Bde
          7.   Tpt Cpl
          8.   W. Diary
          9.   File.

SECRET.   Copy No......

The Gordon Highlanders.

Ref. Sheet: OPERATION ORDER No. 284   30th Oct. 1918.
51 A.
1/40,000.

1. In continuation of Warning Order issued to-day, the Battalion
   will move by route march to THUN-ST.-MARTIN, to-day.

2. **Orders for March:**
   Starting Point   - Cross roads at I.20.c.3.7.
   Time   - 13.30 hours.
   Route   - Road through I.25. and I.31.a. to main road
                      at I.6.b.2.3 - Track to HAVRAIN - Road through
                      I.23 and 29 to IWUY - Road through T.5. and T.1. -
                      THUN ST. MARTIN.
   Order of March   - Bn. H. Qrs., A, B, C, D Coys.
   Interval   - 100 yards between Companies.
   Dress   - Marching Order.

3. **Transport** will move under the orders of Transport Officer as follows:
   Starting Point   - Cross roads at I.20.d.1.0.
   Time   - 13.30 hours.
   Route   - I.32.b.1.6 - Main Road to IWUY via Piave
                      de Valenciennes - THUN ST. MARTIN.
   Distance   - 50 yds. between sections of 12 vehicles.

4. **Billeting Party** has proceeded under Lieut. J.C. MILLER.

5. Blankets and Baggage will be ready for collection at 13.00 hours.
   Blankets will be rolled in bundles of 10 and dumped at Coy Billets;
   a guard will be left and Transport will be sent back for collection
   of blankets this afternoon.
   Mess kits will be dumped at Coy Messes and will be collected at
   13.00 hours.

6. **Acknowledge.**

                                              (signed) A.Risk,   Captain & Adjt.,
                                                       6/7th Bn., The Gordon Highlanders.

Issued at 12.35 hours.

Distribution:-
   Copies 1 - 4.   O.C. Coys.
          5.   Quartermaster.
          6.   Transport Officer.
          7.   O. I/c. Bn. H. Qrs.
          8.   Brig. Mess.
          9.   152nd Inf. Bde.
         10.   War Diary.
         11.   File.

CONFIDENTIAL

War Diary
of
6/7th Battalion, The Gordon Highlanders.

For Period

1st November 1918   30th November 1918.

Volume 49.

Confidential.

WAR DIARY
or
INTELLIGENCE SUMMARY.

(Erase heading not required.)

Army Form C. 2118.

Instructions regarding War Diaries and Intelligence Summaries are contained in F.S. Regs., Part II. and the Staff Manual respectively. Title pages will be prepared in manuscript.

Place	Date	Hour	Summary of Events and Information	Remarks and references to Appendices
THUN LEVEQUE	1.11.18.		Battalion still in THUN LEVEQUE. Men engaged cleaning up kit and equipment, also billets and surroundings, digging latrines etc. Divisional Band played selections for our entertainment during part of the afternoon.	
do.	2.11.18.		Battalion remains in present Billets. Inspections and cleaning up under Company Commanders supervision.	
do.	3.11.18.		Battalion remains in present billets. Church Parades held for all denominations.	
do.	4.11.18.		Battalion remains in present billets. Usual training carried out.	
do.	5.11.18.		Battalion remains in present billets. Usual training and lectures given.	
do.	6.11.18.		Battalion Parade held but as it was very wet, marched back to billets. Health Remained in present billets. Misconduct in Billets Raigo Chief Officer today.	
do.	7.11.18.		Battalion remains in present billets. Captain J.V.F. MACDONALD joined Battalion. "A" Coy. on Range but owing to inclement weather, had to march back to billets.	
do.	8.11.18.		Battalion remains in present billets. Weather threatening rain and men carry on in billets with musketry etc. Tactical Scheme carried out by officers of Brigade. Major MacDONALD assumed duties of Second-in-Command.	
do.	9.11.18.		Battalion remains in present billets. Weather fine and sunny. Parades carried out as per programme - Platoon and Company in attack, etc. & Musketry.	
do.	10.11.18.		Church Parades. Weather splendid.	
do.	11.11.18.		Weather clear and fine. Received news of ARMISTICE signed. Day observed as General Holiday by all troops. "Balmorals" gave their concert to this Brigade in Concert Hall at THUN LEVEQUE. Very successful. Battalion lit great bonfire.	

Army Form C. 2118.

WAR DIARY
or
INTELLIGENCE SUMMARY.
(Erase heading not required.)

Instructions regarding War Diaries and Intelligence Summaries are contained in F. S. Regs., Part II. and the Staff Manual respectively. Title pages will be prepared in manuscript.

Place	Date	Hour	Summary of Events and Information	Remarks and references to Appendices
THUN LEVEQUE	11.11.18		bonfire at 20.30 hours. Slight drizzle all evening.	
do.	12.11.18		Weather clear and sunny. Company Training 09.00 to 10.30 hours, then Companies broke off to prepare ground for sports to be held to-morrow. G.O.C., Divn. spoke to Battalion at 11.00 hours.	
do.	13.11.18		Weather fine and sunny, frost at night. Divisional Cross-Country Run of 3 miles. Holiday in celebration of BEAUMONT HAMEL Battle. Sports in afternoon. Battln. Concert and prize giving in evening. Great success.	
do.	14.11.18		Fine and sunny. Parades - one hour in close order drill and practice in forming three's, to 13.30. Route march - march discipline good.	
do.	15.11.18		Fine and sunny. - frost early morning. Pipe Band and "C" Company proceeded to IWUY as Guard of Honour to Marshal FOCH at 12.00 hrs. Remainder of Battln. (less two platoons on burials and salvage) close order drill 09.00 - 10.30 hrs., afterwards cleaning and fitting up. Guard of Honour inspected by Commander-in-Chief and highly complimented on their steadiness and turnout. Later inspected by Marshal FOCH who also complimented them. Pipe Band remained after inspection to play during lunch. Letter following letter received:- "The Officer Commanding, 6/7th Gordon Highlanders. "The Commander-in-Chief was very well pleased with the turn out of "C" Company of your unit which formed the Guard of Honour for Marshal FOCH. "He said that this Company was the equal of any Company which he had "seen in pre-war days and was certainly one of the best he had seen in "FRANCE. "Your pipers and drummer's gave great satisfaction, and instead of being "dismissed with the Company, were retained to play during lunch." (Signed) A. R. RYAN, Staff Captain, 152nd Infantry Brigade.	
do.	16.11.18		"17.11.18.	

- 3 -

Army Form C. 2118.

WAR DIARY
or
INTELLIGENCE SUMMARY.
(Erase heading not required.)

Instructions regarding War Diaries and Intelligence Summaries are contained in F. S. Regs. Part II, and the Staff Manual respectively. Title pages will be prepared in manuscript.

Place	Date	Hour	Summary of Events and Information	Remarks and references to Appendices
THUN L'EVEQUE	16.11.18		Fine and sunny, sharp frost morning. Battalion Parade - 09.00 - 09.45. Company training. Battn. Cross-Country Run at 14.30 hrs.	
do.	17.11.18		Fine but cold. Church Parade at IWUY - 700 only. "A" and "B" Coys. attended. Commander-in-Chief attended the parade and took March Past afterwards of 152nd and 153rd Infantry Brigades.	
do.	18.11.18		Fine. Parades till 11.00. Lecture by Lieut. SIMCON on "States of Germany before the war". Afternoon, M.M. Ribbons presented to 12 other ranks of the Battn. Afternoon, baseide Football for "A" and "B" Coys. and "Hare and Hounds Run" for "C" & "D" Coys.	
do.	19.11.18		Fine and sunny. Battln. Parades. Prince OBERT visited the Battln. at 11.30 hrs. Battalion en masse did arm drill and march past. Prince expressed his admiration and satisfaction of the turn out. The Prince and his A.D.C. in Headquarters Mess. Left Battln. about 12.45 hours. Battalion at Baths during afternoon.	
do.	20.11.18		Thick mist all day.	
do.	21.11.18		Fine and sunny. Afternoon, training for Sports.	
do.	22.11.18		Fine and sunny, frost early morning. Battalion route march. Rev. BUNCE, C.F., Joined. 2/Lt. A. PHILIP (T.O.) and 2/Lt. A.T. CHEYNE went on leave.	
do.	23.11.18		Very fine and sunny. Battalion Parades. Lecture by Lieut. HAY on Objects and Organisation of Educational Scheme. G.O.C. inspected all Horses in 5th Seaforth Hghrs.' Transport Field.	
do.	24.11.18		Church Parade in Theatre. Fine day.	
do.	25.11.18		Dull day, slight drizzle in forenoon. Battln. on Country Training. Lvt. General called. Lieut. PETERSON went on leave. Captain LINDSAY to PARIS LEAVE and Captain PETERSON to Hospital.	
do.	26.11.18			

Army Form C. 2118.

- 4 -

WAR DIARY
or
INTELLIGENCE-SUMMARY.
(Erase heading not required.)

Instructions regarding War Diaries and Intelligence Summaries are contained in F.S. Regs., Part II. and the Staff Manual respectively. Title pages will be prepared in manuscript.

Place	Date	Hour	Summary of Events and Information	Remarks and references to Appendices
THUN LEVEQUE	26.11.18		Fine and sunny and warm. Battalion Bathing Day. Afternoon - recreational training, very good. Lecture, 17.30, by Rev. GILLISON on "Demobilisation and Reorganisation."	
do.	27.11.18		Dull morning, cleared later. Afternoon - Commencement Divisional Sports. Heats being run off, etc. 11.30 hrs. Lecture to all officers and N.C.Os. by Commanding Officer on "Advance Guards". Sports - 3rd place in relay race, knocked out in everything else except wrestling on horseback. 5 a-side lost - 3. - 0.	
do.	28.11.18		Advanced Guard Scheme March cancelled. Heavy rain. Afternoon - Lecture by Adjutant on "Discipline and Behaviour on march to and in New Area". Divisional Cinema opened in Theatre here to-night.	
do.	29.11.18		Dull. Battalion Parades. Lecture to Battalion by Major WATT on "The Daily Press". Recreational training off in afternoon. Advance Parties to new billetting area did not go at last minute. Go to-morrow.	
do.	30.11.18		General Holiday. Divisional Sports and St. Andrew's Day. Fine day. 7th Black Watch Divisional Champions. We won individual and team dancing. Night Concert in Theatre by 152nd Brigade. Great success. Extras issued at night - Porridge, Beer, and Rum-punch.	
do.			Honours awarded during the month:-	
			THE MILITARY CROSS 8	
			THE DISTINGUISHED CONDUCT MEDAL ... 2	
			Bar to THE MILITARY MEDAL 3	
			THE MILITARY MEDAL 27	
do.			Strength/	

Army Form C. 2118.

WAR DIARY
INTELLIGENCE SUMMARY.
(Erase heading not required.)

Place	Date	Hour	Summary of Events and Information	Remarks and references to Appendices
THUN LEVEEQUE	30.M.N.		STRENGTH at end of last month......... Officers. 42 Other Ranks. 730	
			INCREASE : Reinforcements............ 9 432	
			51 1162	
			DECREASE : Casualties and Evacuated.... 4 35	
			STRENGTH at end of this month......... 47 1127	

Macdonald, Major,
Commanding 6/7th Batt'n. The Gordon Highlanders.

CONFIDENTIAL

WAR DIARY

OF

6/7th Battalion, The Gordon Highlanders

From 1st to 31st December, 1918.

(VOLUME 50)

Confidential.   **WAR DIARY** or **INTELLIGENCE SUMMARY.**

Army Form C. 2118.

(Erase heading not required.)

Instructions regarding War Diaries and Intelligence Summaries are contained in F.S. Regs., Part II. and the Staff Manual respectively. Title pages will be prepared in manuscript.

Place	Date	Hour	Summary of Events and Information	Remarks and references to Appendices
THUN LEVEQUE	Dec. 1st		Fine but cold. Church Parade. 12.30 hours - Parade for Promulgation of a Field General Court Martial. Lieut. T.W. STEWART, MC. joined. Capt. & Q.M. F.W. FINDLAY, MC. went on special leave.	/hr.
"	2nd		Fine. Battalion Advance Guard Scheme - "A" Coy. Advance Guard. Afternoon - Inter-Company Football League started to find players. "B" Coy. held a Concert. Lieut. A.J.W. CARNIE, MC., joined.	/hr.
"	3rd		Wet day. Companies filling in particulars of Industrial Groups and employment &c. Lecture at 11.30 hours on "RHODESIA" by Lieut. McGREGOR, A. & S. Hdrs. Good, but rather beyond the men, as apparently you require £1,000 in your pocket before going out there!!	/hr.
"	4th		Wet morning, cleared 11.00 hours. Platoons under Platoon Commanders. 11.30 hours - Lecture by Adjutant on OUTPOSTS. Afternoon - Inter-Platoon Football League. Run for remainder.	/hr.
"	5th		Fine. Companies doing Outpost Scheme except "B" Coy on Range. Classes as usual. Lieut.-Colonel G.J.B. CRANSTOUN came back to the Battalion from Commanding the Brigade to-day. Captain G.T. BURNEY, 4th Gordon Highlanders, posted to this Battalion.	/hr.
"	6th		Very fine. Battalion Route March - seven miles. Classes as usual. Captain R. RISK, MC., proceeded to CALAIS and Home on duty - first getting NCOs. from the Base, and Home for the Battalion Colours. Major J. GRAN rejoined from leave. Brought news of the death of Captain W.J.C. FLEMING from 'flu. Inter-Company Football Matches.	/hr.
"	7th		Dull day. Battalion at Baths. Two Company Football Games - "D" V. "B" in morning and HQ. V. "B" in afternoon. Very fine afternoon. Second soccer game a draw - 1 goal each. Fine/	/hr.

Army Form C. 2118.

WAR DIARY
or
INTELLIGENCE SUMMARY
(Erase heading not required.)

Instructions regarding War Diaries and Intelligence Summaries are contained in F. S. Regs., Part II. and the Staff Manual respectively. Title pages will be prepared in manuscript.

Place	Date	Hour	Summary of Events and Information	Remarks and references to Appendices
TAUN LEVEQUE	Dec 7.			
	8th.		Fine Day. Church Parade attended by Brigadier General Commanding who took March Past. Lieut. R.G. LINDSAY, MC., back from PARIS PLAGE. Colour Party left for UNITED KINGDOM:- Captain R. RISK, MC. Lieut. A.J.W. CARNIE, MC. Lieut. J.L. RAITT C Coy. 265154 CSM J.W. Chalmers, MC., DCM., MM. D " 266247 Sgt W. Legge A " 265114 Sgt J.C. Sutherland. A " 265003 Pte J. Smith, MM B " 265181 Pte W. McLean.	M.
"	9th.		Dull morning. Battalion Parade. Company Advance Guard Schemes. Battalion Inter-Platoon Leagues in afternoon. Classes as usual. "B" Company on Range.	M.
"	10th.		Dull and cold. Battalion Parade and Company work. Lecture "Canada" after the "War" cancelled. 12.00 hours heavy rain. Leagues put off till 14.30 hours when weather cleared. Only 5 games played. Major J. Cran to Hospital for operation. "C" Company on Range.	M.
"	11th.		Very wet morning. Battalion Parade cut short. Platoons at disposal of Platoon Commanders. "A" versus "B" Company at football in afternoon. "A" Company won - 2 goals against 1. - Good Game. 17.30 hours - Battalion Sports Meeting.	M.
"	12th.		Wet morning. Route-March cancelled. Platoons under Platoon Commanders. Very heavy rain till 11.30 hours. Arm Drill under R.S.M. Afternoon - Football Leagues. Rugby game with R.E. Lecture 5.30 by Major WILLCOCKS on "Battle of FAMARS 1793".	M.
"	13th.		Battalion Parade. Dry, high wind all day. Usual training. Officers versus Sergeants Football Match. Officers won 3 - 1.	M.

Army Form C. 2118.

WAR DIARY
OF
INTELLIGENCE SUMMARY.
(Erase heading not required.)

Instructions regarding War Diaries and Intelligence Summaries are contained in F. S. Regs., Part II. and the Staff Manual respectively. Title pages will be prepared in manuscript.

Place	Date	Hour	Summary of Events and Information	Remarks and references to Appendices
THUN LEVEQUE	Oct. 14th		Very fine and sunny. Battalion Parade. Companies at disposal of Company Commanders. Battalion 1st XI v. 5th Seaforth Highlanders 1st XI -- lost 3 - 2. Very good game.	
"	15th		Church Parade. G.O.C. Division, attended. Fine day. Party sent off to-day to buy Christmas Stores.	
"	16th		Fine. Battalion Parade as per programme. Afternoon - Football League.	
"	17th		Baths. Later, Baths reported off. Companies under Company Commanders. Showers. Afternoon - various games.	
"	18th		High wind, showers. No Battalion Parades. Lt. Col. C. J. E. CRANSTOUN left at 09.30 hours on leave to south of FRANCE, after "flu". Lecture on Education by Captain ALLARDYCE, 6th Argyll & Sutherland Highlanders. Good and instructive. Battalion Matches off.	
"	19th		Heavy showers. Battalion Parade off. Companies on Advance Guard Scheme. Captain G.T. BURNEY, MC, to proceed to 1st Battalion, The Gordon Highlanders. R.G.C. held Meeting re Salvage at 17.30. Very wet night.	
"	20th		Battalion Route March. Fine morning. G.O.C. 232nd Transport, Battalion Rugby XV versus M.G.C. XV. Loss 6 - 0. Good game. Captain G.T. BURNEY, MC. proceeded to 1st Battalion this morning. Captain & Q.M. F.W. FINDLAY, MC., returned from leave.	
"	21st		Baths. First and second XI s ver as 6th Seaforth Highlanders. First Battalion lost 4 - 0, Second won - 1 - 0. Major W.H. NEWSON, MC. reported to Battalion.	
"	22nd		Church Parade.	
"	23rd		Showers. Whole Battalion on salvage work till 13.00 hours. Captain R. RISK, MC. and Colour Party returned to-day. M.O. left for MENTONE on French leave.	

Army Form C. 2118.

WAR DIARY
or
INTELLIGENCE SUMMARY.

(Erase heading not required.)

Instructions regarding War Diaries and Intelligence Summaries are contained in F. S. Regs., Part II. and the Staff Manual respectively. Title pages will be prepared in manuscript.

Place	Date	Hour	Summary of Events and Information	Remarks and references to Appendices
THUN LEVEQUE	Dec. 24th.		Very fine. Battalion on Salvage work – Battalion Area cleared and dumps of shells formed on road sides.	
"	25th.		Christmas Day. General Holiday. Extra dinner for men. Football Matches in morning and afternoon. Concert in evening. Very fine.	
"	26th.		Boxing Day. General Holiday, except for Duty Company who were out on Salvage.	
"	27th.		Very wet day. All parades off. 11.00 hours lecture by Lieut. MACKENZIE, 4th Seaforth Highlanders on "Agricultural Organisation" – very good.	
"	28th.		Battalion Parade and Ceremonial Drill. Three Commanding officers of Brigade to new area to look round. Very wet day.	
"	29th.		Church Parades. Tug-of-War versus 6th Seaforth Highlanders – lost both Cat on and Light Weights. Showery day.	
"	30th.		Fine. Battalion practise Ceremonial Drill, Arm Drill, &c. Platoon Football.(Commanding officers' Conference at Brigade).	
"	31st.		Showers. General Holiday. Divisional Cross-Country run, 3½ miles. Battalion Concert by officers in evening. Rum issue. Concert attend by Brigadier General Commanding and his Brigade Major. B.G.C. greeted with great cheers. Concert a huge success, finished at 24.00 hours. New Year brought in with "Auld Lang Syne" and cheers. Pipe Band played round village.	

	OFFICERS	O.Rs.
Strength at end of last month	47	1127
INCREASE: Reinforcements, Casuals &c.	4	117
	51	1244
DECREASE: Casualties, Evacuated Sick, Miners &c. to U.K.	3	133
Strength at end of this month	48	1111

HONOURS/

Army Form C. 2118.

WAR DIARY
or
INTELLIGENCE SUMMARY.

(Erase heading not required.)

- 5 -

Instructions regarding War Diaries and Intelligence Summaries are contained in F. S. Regs., Part II. and the Staff Manual respectively. Title pages will be prepared in manuscript.

Place	Date	Hour	Summary of Events and Information	Remarks and references to Appendices
THUN L'EVEQUE	Oct 31st		HONOURS & AWARDS.	
			Bar to MILITARY CROSS - 1.	
			DISTINGUISHED CONDUCT MEDAL - 2.	
			Mentioned in Despatches - 5 Officers & 2 Other Ranks.	

Macdonald
Major,
Commanding 6/7th Bn., The Gordon Highlanders.

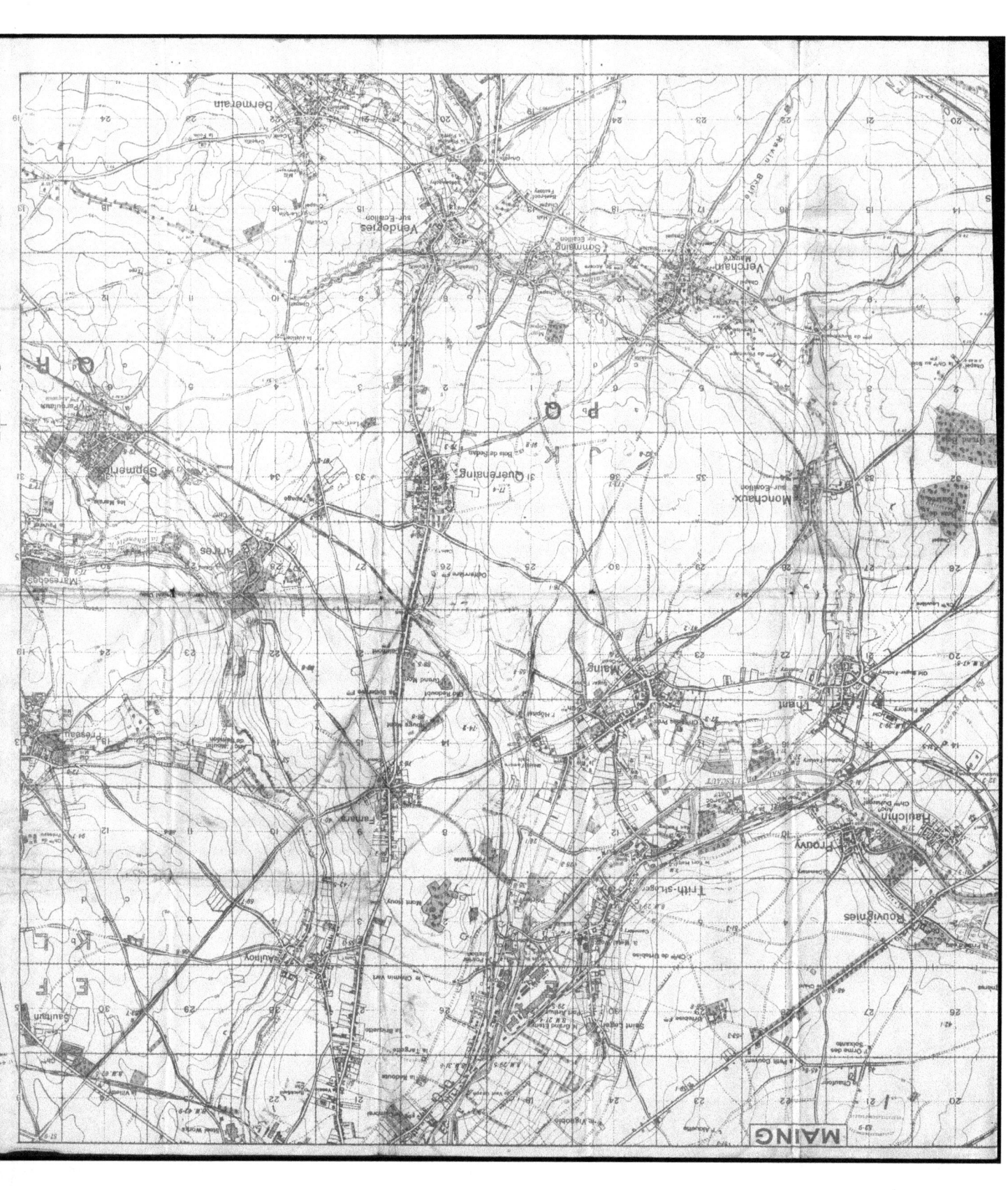

WAR DIARY
or
INTELLIGENCE SUMMARY.
(Erase heading not required.)

Army Form C. 2118.

Instructions regarding War Diaries and Intelligence Summaries are contained in F. S. Regs., Part II. and the Staff Manual respectively. Title pages will be prepared in manuscript.

Place	Date	Hour	Summary of Events and Information	Remarks and references to Appendices
THUN-LEVEQUE.	January 1919.			
	1.		New Year's Day. General Holiday. Extra dinner for troops. Men doing their own amusements, mostly recovering from the night before. Fine day. Captain McLeod returned from leave.	
	2.		Battalion Ceremonial Parade. High wind. Capt. R. Risk to Hospital – Cold and Rash. Lieut. Carney to Headquarters as Assistant Adjutant. Lieut. Hay on leave.	
	3.		G.O.C's. Inspection and presentation of Medals. Took the form of a Guard of Honour and presentation of Medals in Concert Hall – Very Good Show and General very well pleased. Fine day but ground too slippery to put up an outside Review.	
	4.		Wet day. General holiday. Rugby Team played D.M.G.at IVUY in League Championship and won 8 – 3 points – scrappy game.	
	5.		Sunday. Baths and Church Parade. Battalion Association Team versus 5th Seaforths in Brigade League – lost 3 – 1. Ground in a very bad state indeed. The Tug-of-War Catch and Light weights we won because 5th Seaforths Team did not turn up.	
	6.		Fine day. Transport left this Area for forward Area. Battalion engaged in clearing up their billets &c.	
HOUDENG-AIMERIES.	7.		Battalion Embussed at 09.30 hours at THUN ST.MARTIN in 40 lorri &c. (25 men each). Convoy left 10.15 hours, arrived at HOUDENG-AIMERIES at 17.30 hours, after dark. Companies settled in by about 19.30 hours. Fine day and Good run up.	
	8.		Very fine day. Battalion settling down in new Billets, and getting to know their way about.	
	9.		Battalion Parade off. Wet Day.	

Army Form C. 2118.

WAR DIARY
or
INTELLIGENCE SUMMARY.
(Erase heading not required.)

Place	Date	Hour	Summary of Events and Information	Remarks and references to Appendices
	January 1919			
	10.		Battalion Route March. Fine day.	
	11.		Holiday. Fine day.	
	12.		Church Parades. Fine day. Battalion played 5th Seaforths in Brigade League - lost 1 - 0. HOUDENG AIMERIES Stake Band played selections to Brigade during the afternoon in the Town Band Stand.	
	13.		Battalion Parades - Army Drill, P.T. &c. Fine day.	
	14.		Battalion Parades. Coy. Commanders rode over Salvage Area allotted the Battalion. Area quite clear. Afternoon match versus 5th Seaforths who did not turn up. Tug-of-War team lost versus same Battalion. Rugby XV versus 5th Seaforths. Draw 3 points each Scrappy Game.	
	15.		Dull day. Battalion Route March. Afternoon, heavy rain.	
	16.		Very fine and Sunny.	
	17.		Battalion Parades. Commanding Officer and Second in Command went to Brussels. Rain all day.	
	18.		Saturday. Holiday. Battalion at Baths.	
	19.		Church Parades. Fine day. Brigade Massed Pipers played at BOIS DE LUC.	
	20.		Very fine. Frost. Battalion Parades.	
	21.		Very fine. Frost. Battalion Route March - Very good one.	
	22.		Very fine. Hard Frost. Battalion Parades.	

Army Form C. 2118.

WAR DIARY
or
INTELLIGENCE SUMMARY.
(Erase heading not required.)

Place	Date	Hour	Summary of Events and Information	Remarks and references to Appendices
	January 1919. 23.		Very fine. Battalion Parades and Route March.	
	24.		Very fine.	
	25.		Holiday. Officers versus Sergeants soccer match. Officers won 3-1. Warrant Officers and Sergeants gave a Burns Night Dinner, Commanding Officer, Second-in-Command, Adjutant, 4 Company Commanders, Transport Officer, Quartermaster, Officer i/c Bn. Headquarters, Medical Officer present. Splendid night. Two of our Pipers (Pipe Major I. Howarth and Piper G. Forbes) went with a Divisional Pipe Band (12 players; each Battalion being represented) to play at a BURNS Night Concert at the Albert Hall, London.	3
	26.		Snow. Church Parades. Lieut-Colonel C.J.E.Cranstoun DSO returned to the Battalion and resumed command. Battalion Commanders Conference at Brigade Headquarters at 16.30 hours.	
	27.		Battalion Parade. Snow and hard frost. Battalion doing P.T. and Games.	
	28.		Snow. Route March cancelled owing to state of roads. More snow and frost. Major Macdonald and Major Nawson to Brussel's to attend Allied Corps Court Ball. Prince of Wales visited the Battalion, spoke to various men and inspected some Billets. Went Headquarters Mess for Tea, but couldn't stay.	
	29.		Battalion Parade. P.T.&c. Snow and Frost.	
	30.		Battalion at Baths.	
	31.		Battalion Parade. P.T.&c. Ground too hard and slippery to do any-thing. Very cold.	

Peter Mulvey Captain.
Commanding 6/7th Battalion, THE GORDON HIGHLANDERS.

CONFIDENTIAL

WAR DIARY

OF

6/7th Battalion, The Gordon Highlanders

For Period

1st February 1919   28th February, 1919.

VOLUME 52.

Army Form C. 2118.

WAR DIARY
INTELLIGENCE SUMMARY.
(Erase heading not required.)

Instructions regarding War Diaries and Intelligence Summaries are contained in F.S. Regs., Part II. and the Staff Manual respectively. Title pages will be prepared in manuscript.

Place	Date	Hour	Summary of Events and Information	Remarks and references to Appendices
HUDDING-ALMERIES	February 1919.			
	1.		Holiday. A party of 110 being got ready for demobilization for Monday.	
	2.		Church Parades. Fine.	
	3.		Fine. Party of 110 under Lieutenants J.Collier and R.M. Norrice, and 2nd Lieutenants A. & J.Brunskill and J.Davidson left 9 a.m. for demobilization. Battalion Parades, P.T. &c. Hard Frost. Cold but Fine - Captain D.McDuff went on leave.	
	4.		Train Guard Party left. Lecture on Electricity. Commanding Officer takes over Command of Brigade. Dull and Snowing. Cold.	
	5.		Major MacDonald goes on leave. Captain F.V.Mulvey in Command. Lecture on Physical Training. Hard Frost Continues.	
	6.		Battalion at Games. Lecture by Lieut-Colonel C.J.E.Grayson DSO. to all officers on advantages in forming Army of Occupation.	
	7.		Battalion Parade and P.T. Lecture by the Revd.M.T.Irvine C.F. on "Ballads of Scotland". This was much appreciated by the Battalion.	
	8.		Holiday. Party of 33 under 2nd Lieut. W.I.Cheyne for demobilization.	
	9.		Church Parades. Conference of Officers Commanding Companies re anticipation of Companies and arrangements for Cadre. Captn. J.McLeod, Lieutenants C.M.Cowie, E.Rector MC., and A.Philip left for Demobilization. Hard Frost.	
	10.		Battalion parade and P.T. Cold. Captain R.Ridler MC. to arms. with official photograph.	

Army Form C. 2118.

→ Sheet 2.

WAR DIARY
or
INTELLIGENCE SUMMARY.
(Erase heading not required.)

Instructions regarding War Diaries and Intelligence
Summaries are contained in F.S. Regs., Part II.
and the Staff Manual respectively. Title pages
will be prepared in manuscript.

Place	Date	Hour	Summary of Events and Information	Remarks and references to Appendices
HOUDENG AIMERIES.	February 1919.			
	11.		Battalion Parade and P.T. Right Half of Battalion beat Left Half of Battalion, at Football by 2 goals to one.	
	12.		Battalion Parade and P.T. Lt-Colonel C.J.E.Cranston DSO. went off to Bethune to visit our Detachment.	
	13.		Battalion at Baths. Clear cold Weather.	
	14.		Battalion on P.T. Captain R.Black MC.returns. Lieut.F.Pemberthy and party of 40 Other Ranks leave for Demobilization. Change in weather, fresh and raining.	
	15.		General Holiday. Interview of party of 84 Other Ranks, leaving for Demobilization. Lt-Colonel C.J.E.Cranston DSO.resumes Command. Mild fresh weather. Snow disappearing.	
	16.		Church Parades. Lieutenants D.Peterson, T.W.Stewart MC., V.L. Davies, and A.Roe MM., with 85 men went off for Demobilization.	
	17.		Battalion Parades and re-organisation of Companies into two Platoons.	
	18.		Battalion Parade and P.T. Weather improving.	
	19.		Battalion preparing for sending Draft to 1/4th Battalion, The Gordon Highlanders. No Parades.	
	20.		90 men left for 1/4th Battalion, The Gordon Highlanders, under Captain P.V.McIvey, 2nd Lieutenants A.Robertson, W.Harold and J.J.Fowler. 60 men from 1/4th Bn. The Gordon Highlanders arrive No Parades. Weather dry and springlike.	

Army Form C. 2118.

WAR DIARY
or
INTELLIGENCE SUMMARY.
(Erase heading not required.)

Instructions regarding War Diaries and Intelligence Summaries are contained in F. S. Regs., Part II. and the Staff Manual respectively. Title pages will be prepared in manuscript.

Place	Date	Hour	Summary of Events and Information	Remarks and references to Appendices
HUDDING ARMERIES	February 1919. 21.		Re-organization commenced. In the afternoon orders were received that 1st Bn. The Gordon Highlanders draft was cancelled and would proceed to the 1/4th Bn., The Gordon Highlanders, leaving with that Battalion for Germany the following morning. Reimbure party returned.	
	22.		1st Bn. The Gordon Highlanders party left at 7.30 a.m. under 2Lt John H. Bisson Bn. Later word was received that train had left, and party was being put up for the night at Menage.	
	23.		1/4th Bn., The Gordon Highlanders with men joining from this Bn. left Menage at 11 a.m. Church Service.	
	24.		No orders for London Scottish Draft. Companies at the disposal of Company Commanders.	
	25.		31 men for demobilization interviewed.	
	26.		Party for demobilization left under Captain W.N.Newson MC and Lieut. W.A.Syers. In the morning Battalion attended a lecture in the "Blumeris" Theatre.	
	27.		Battalion at Baths.	
	28.		Wet and drizzly. Companies at the disposal of Company Commanders	

Commanding 6/7th Battalion, THE GORDON HIGHLANDERS.

Lieut-Colonel

6/4 Gordons 11 ~

Army Form C. 2118.

WAR DIARY
*
INTELLIGENCE SUMMARY.
(Erase heading not required.)

Instructions regarding War Diaries and Intelligence Summaries are contained in F. S. Regs., Part II. and the Staff Manual respectively. Title pages will be prepared in manuscript.

Place	Date	Hour	Summary of Events and Information	Remarks and references to Appendices
HOUDENG AIMERIES	March 1919. 1st		Beautiful Spring Day. General Holiday. Draft of 23 for Demobilization left. Party sent to funeral of Private J. Brown (Headquarter Runner) and Private Barr.	
	2nd		Weather very fine. Church Parades.	
	3rd		Wet and Stormy. Companies at disposal of Company Commanders	
	4th		Weather wet. No parades.	
	5th		Weather warm and fine. Thunder in evening. Companies at the disposal of Company Commanders.	
	6th		Very wet. Lieutenant H. GRAY MC. and party leave for Base. Battalion at Baths.	
	7th		Dry and cold. Lieutenants R.G. Lindsay and R. Henry return from leave. Captain R. Risk MC. and CQMS. Keir and three men leave on Demobilization.	
	8th		Wet. Commanding Officer on leave. Major Macdonald in Command. Party of 11 Other Ranks to 1/4th Bn., The Gordon Highlanders Captain D. MacDuff returns from leave.	
	9th		Weather improving? Brigade Church Parade.	
	10th		Cold and windy. Companies at the disposal of Company Commanders. 2nd Lieut. E.S. Macdonald returns from Course;	
	11th		Beautiful bright first day. Fatigues on Football ground. Six Horses leave for Base.	
	12th		Weather very good. Captain Findlay MC. goes to Hospital. 50 men on Coal Fatigue.	

Army Form C. 2118.

WAR DIARY
or
INTELLIGENCE SUMMARY.
(Erase heading not required.)

Sheet 2

Place	Date	Hour	Summary of Events and Information	Remarks and references to Appendices
HOUDENG AIMERIES	March 1919.			
	13th		Weather very good. Battalion at Baths.	
	14th		Exellent weather. Medical Inspection of Draft. Company at disposal of Officers Commanding Companies.	
	15th		Wether very good. Completion of drafts papers.	
	16th		Weather exellent. Draft for 1/4th Bn., The Gordon Highlanders leaves/ 8 Officers and 129 Other Ranks. Lieutenant H. Gray MC returns from Horse Conducting.	
	17th		Good weather. Lieutenants W. Weir MC. and J. Anderson return. Surplus men on Fatigues.	
	18th		Weather exellent. Captain D. MacDuff billeting in Manage.	
	19th		Weather very good. Lieutenants W. Weir and J. Anderson and 2 Other Ranks leave for 1/4th Bn., The Gordon Highlanders.	
	20th		Exellent weather. Battalion at Baths. Dining Hall and reading room cleared of tables and forms. Preparations for move of Transport.	
	21st		Good weather. Transport moves to Manage. 2nd Lieutenant H. McN. Allan reports for duty.	
	22nd		Exellent weather. Major Newson returns from leave. Captain Maltby MC. proceeds on leave to the U.K.	
	23rd		Weather good. Lieutenant H. McNallan proceeds to 1/4th Bn., The Gordon Highlanders. Captain New	
	24th		Cold and dry. Battalion moves to FAYT. Checking of Stores begins by Quartermaster/	

Army Form C. 2118.

WAR DIARY
or
INTELLIGENCE SUMMARY.
(Erase heading not required.)

Instructions regarding War Diaries and Intelligence Summaries are contained in F. S. Regs., Part II. and the Staff Manual respectively. Title pages will be prepared in manuscript.

Place	Date	Hour	Summary of Events and Information	Remarks and references to Appendices
HOUDENG AIMERIES	March 1919.			
	25th		Cold and stormy. Major Macdonald goes on leave. 11 Horses leave for Machine Gun Battalion.	
	26th		Improved weather. Last 8 horses leave for Base. Commanding Officer visits Boels Factory Guard. Checking of Stores continues.	
	27th		Cold and stormy. 2 men leave Demobilized. 2 Clerks leave for Base. Lieutenant W.Sayers returns and proceeds on Demobilization.	
	28th		Wet, cold weather. Commanding Officer at General Court Martial. 2 men leave for 1/4th Bn.,The Gordon Highlanders. Captain W.Newson MC. leaves for Demobilization.	
	29th		Weather improving. 4 men leave for 1/4th Bn., The Gordon Highlanders. Battalion paid out.	
	30th		Good Weather. Checking of stores continues.	
	31st		Excellent weather. All surplus men at Baths. Escorts for 2 prisoners despatched.	

D.M.Duff Captain,

Commanding 6/7th Bn.,The Gordon Highlanders.

1/6TH BATTALION, GORDON HIGHLANDERS.

1918.   Appendix.

March   FREMICOURT

1st   Companies at the disposal of   Reference
             Company Commanders for   Map
             inspection of Trench Kit,   57C.1/40,000
             and preparing for the line.   O.0.169
             Battalion moved off from camp
             at 7.45 p.m., 100 yards interval
             between platoons. Guides were
             met at post 20 (J.10.a.3.3.)
             and the relief of the 4th
             Gordon Highlanders commenced
             and was completed at 12.30 a.m.
             The Battalion occupies the
             Brigade Centre Sector Left Sub.
             Sector, running from
             D.20.c.8.4. left to J.6.a.5.2.
             right. "D" Company LEFT front,
             "B" Company RIGHT front, "C"
             Company SUPPORT, and "A" Company
             RESERVE. Battalion Headquarters
             at J.10.b.0.7.

             IN TRENCHES

2nd   Forenoon spent reconnoitring Front
             line and Defensive posts. Work
             of wiring Sunken Road, J.4.3.b.1. -
             J.5.c.0.3. arranged for when dark.
             2 Officers and 100 men employed.
             Weather very cold with intermittent
             snow showers. 450 yards of wire
             put up in afternoon. The work of
             cleaning and repairing Front and
             Support lines went on all day.
             Enemy very quiet all day and
             night. Thickening front wire.

3rd   A dull morning and slight rain.
             Wiring of Sunken Road. Construction
             and improvement of fire bays in
             front and support lines. 800 yards
             of wiring done on Sunken Road
             and BOURSIES. The night passed
             quietly.

4th   Dull, damp, cold morning. Quiet
             night. Owing to the mist
             it was possible to wire the
             reserve line all day and 1100
             yards were completed as well
             as part thickened by "C" Company.
             "D" Company thickened up wire
             opposite No.20 Post. A party
             was also working clearing the
             berm of FISH AVENUE and making
             fire-steps.

5th   Cold dull morning turned into a
             fine drying day. The wiring of
             the reserve line completed in the
             morning. Work on duckboards in
             support line. Revetting firesteps
             in front line and support line.

1918.   Appendix.

March

5th   Digging and enlarging Post 21
(Ctd).   also improving Posts 18 & 19.
           Quiet night.

6th   Frost at night, fine day but hazy
           and visibility bad. Usual work on
           trenches, repairing and making
           firesteps. Enlarging Post 21
           and digging firesteps between
           Posts 19 & 20. Wiring and
           improving trenches. Battalion
           to be relieved to-morrow by the 6th
           Seaforth Highlanders.

7th   The usual work. General ALEXANDER
           of the U.S. Army was taken round
           our trenches and shown everything
           this morning. Owing to a haze the   O.O.170
           relief took place in daylight
           between 4 p.m. and 6 p.m. We had
           two casualties coming out and it
           was very lucky we had not more
           as an eight inch shell burst on
           the CAMBRAI - BAPAUME Road amongst
           a section and only two men were
           wounded. The Battalion is in huts
           at O'SHEA CAMP in Brigade Reserve.

           O'SHEA CAMP

8th   O'SHEA CAMP. Cleaning up and
           improving camp. Company Commanders
           reconnoitring routes and positions
           in Reserve Line.

9th   Battalion at Baths all day.

10th   Church Parade.

11th   "A" & "C" Companies inspected by
           Commanding Officer. All Respirators
           inspected. Reconnoitring Front Line.

12th   All companies inspected by Commanding
           Officer. Officers reconnoitring
           line.

13th   The Battalion moved off to the line,
           the first Company moving off at   O.O.171
           12.30 p.m 300 yards between Sections.
           The Battalion took over Centre
           Battalion Sector from 5th Seaforth
           Highlanders. "A" Company - Front
           Line, "C" Company - Support,
           "B" Company - Intermediate and
           "D" Company - Reserve Line.

14th   All available men in Support and
           Intermediate Lines working 8 hours
           per day on wiring and general trench
           repair.

15th   Weather very fine. Same work as
           yesterday. Party of 75 men carrying
           60 lb. bombs to No Man's Land.

1918.   Appendix.

March

16th   Work as above, enemy quiet.

17th   Work as above, enemy quiet.

18th   Work as above. Enemy registering
        on batteries and DOIGNIES and
        DOIGNIES - DEMICOURT Road.

        IN TRENCHES

19th   Inter-Company relief. "C" Company
        relieved "A" Company in Front
        Line. "B" Company relieved "C"   O.O.172
        Company. "A" Company came back to
        Intermediate Line. Working parties
        suspended on account of relief.

20th   During day men rested. At night
        all available men on working
        parties digging new reserve line
        from J.5.c.1.0. to BOURSIES -
        DOIGNIES Road. Battalion worked
        in two shifts. First from 7.15 p.m.
        to 11.30 p.m., second 11.45 p.m.
        to 3 a.m. Trench completed.

21st   For report on operations from
to   21st to 26th March, 1918 see
26th   Appendix attached hereto.

        NEUVILLETTE

27th   The Battalion were to embus from
        PAS to NEUVILLETTE, but owing to
        the uncertainty of the arrival of
        the buses we were given the option
        of marching about 8 miles which we
        did. Starting at 10.45 a.m. having
        dinners en route from the Cookers
        at POMMERA and arriving at
        NEUVILLETTE at 4.30 p.m. where the
        Battalion was billetted in comfortable
        billets. Indents for kit already
        gone in.

28th   The Battalion resting and cleaning up.
        Some of the fighting equipment
        indented for arrived.

        NEUVILLETTE - LABEUVRIERE

29th   Orders were received to march to
        FREVENT and then to entrain for the
        LILLERS area at 1 p.m. The Battalion O.O.173
        left at 10.15 a.m. Cookers were   O.O.174
        sent on and the men had their
        dinners in a field near the
        station. While resting after
        their dinners the King's car was
        seen coming along the road and
        the Battalion received him with
        tremendous cheering. Whereupon
        His Majesty stopped his car and
        spoke to several officers and

1918.   Appendix.

March

29th   N.C.Os. Then the Battalion was
(Ctd).   marched past the King and His
          Majesty expressed his admiration for
          the appearance of the Battalion and
          his pleasure at having seen them.
          The train left FREVENT at 3.30 p.m.
          and arrived at LAPUGNOY at 6 p.m.
          The Battalion was billetted at
          LABEUVRIERE quite close to the
          Station in good billets.

          LABEUVRIERE

30th   Battalion resting at LABEUVRIERE.

31st   Battalion cleaning up. More equipment
          arrived from the Ordnance.

          HONOURS & AWARDS
              NIL.
                                              Officers O.R.
          Strength at end of last month   42   1012
          ADD:-   Off.O.R.
          Drafts ...   .   -   46
          Casuals...   ...   .   -   15
          Officers joined during month   2 - 2   61
                                                  44   1073
          DEDUCT:-
          Evacuations   98
          To United Kingdom for Commission   -   2
          To Base - Tradesmen   ...   -   2
          To U.K. - Officers' Substitution   2   -
                              Scheme.
          To 51st (S) Battn. M.G.C.   -   9
          Casualties :-
          Killed   )   2   35
          Wounded   ) as Per   11 159
          Unaccounted For   ) Appendix   3   74
          Died of Wounds   )   -   6 18   385

          Strength at end of this month ...   26   688

                              A A DUFF
                                       Major
                         Commanding 6th Gordon Highlanders.

ACCOUNT OF OPERATIONS commencing near
BOURSIES on 21st March, 1918, and
lasting till 26th March, 1918.

21st March, 1918.

4.45 a.m.   Intense bombardment of British lines, Front, Support, and Intermediate lines all being included. Barrage consisted of 8", 5.9" and gas shells.

The QUARRY was barraged and a large number of gas shells fell in and around it.

9.15 a.m.   Enemy seen bombing along STURGEON SUPPORT Trench from direction of BOURSIES. What men were left in Front line were withdrawn to Support line and a block was formed in the trench and the enemy held up.

A platoon from the QUARRY had been moved up and manned STURGEON AVENUE between Sunk Road and STURGEON SUPPORT.

10.15 a.m.   The troops in STURGEON SUPPORT were driven out. Enemy were now in STURGEON AVENUE and tried to bomb down towards BOURSIES - CRUCIFIX Road. A block was made in STURGEON AVENUE and enemy held up.

11 a.m.   Bombs ran short and block was forced down STURGEON AVENUE a short distance.

11.30 a.m.   Enemy in great numbers seen coming from BOURSIES and trying to get down BOURSIES - DOIGNIES Road. Three Lewis Guns and all rifles in STURGEON AVENUE opened fire on them inflicting many casualties. The garrison by this time was forced down STURGEON AVENUE some eighty yards south of BOURSIES - CRUCIFIX Road and a block established there. More bombs and rifle grenades arrived from Battalion Headquarters and enemy were again held up for about an hour.

1.30 p.m.   Owing to increasing enemy pressure from front and left flank the block in STURGEON had again to fall back about seventy yards below the QUARRY. This position was held till orders were received to withdraw at 1.30 a.m. on 22nd March, 1918.

The platoon at J.5.c.1.0. on CAMBRAI Road were nearly all taken prisoners. They held their position till nearly surrounded and then only the officer and four men got away down the BOURSIES - DOIGNIES Road to the Intermediate Line.

"A" Company and two platoons of "D" Company in the Intermediate Line were heavily shelled and gassed. When enemy were seen coming out of BOURSIES they were ordered to counter-attack, but, owing to the heavy machine gun fire from the hedge in front of the Reserve line the attack was held up. After this "A" Company lost touch on their left flank and withdrew and formed a defensive flank South of DOIGNIES which was shortly afterwards occupied by the enemy. This line was held till 1.30 a.m.

The remaining two platoons of "D" Company who were in reserve at LEBUCQUIERE held a part of the BEAUMETZ - MORCHIES line South of the BAPAUME - CAMBRAI Road till 2 a.m. on the 23rd March, 1918.

22nd March, 1918.

At 1.30 a.m. the battalion was ordered to take up a position along the plank Road in J.19. and D.20.c. and remained there till 1.30 p.m. when orders were received to hold a line on the North side of the BAPAUME - CAMBRAI Road covering BEUGNY.

At 3 p.m. orders were received to proceed to MIDDLESEX CAMP where the battalion had a hot meal.

At 5.30 p.m. the battalion was ordered to form a line along the railway 1500 yards North of FREMICOURT facing BEUGNATRE.

23rd March, 1918.

At 1 a.m. the battalion was withdrawn to MIDDLESEX CAMP when a hot meal was provided for the men and where Echelon B joined the battalion.

At 12 noon orders were received to take up a position on a line 200 yards North and South of MILL CROSS facing LEBUCQUIERE; the line North of MILL CROSS was astride the FREMICOURT - LEBUCQUIERE Road. This line was 600 yards from the Green line. The orders were to reinforce Green line if necessary and hold our line. The line was held in section posts- "B" and "C" Companies in Front line, "A" and "D" Companies in support. This position was intermittently shelled during the afternoon and evening.

At 4 p.m. orders were received that the battalion was attached to the 56th Brigade and under orders of the Officer Commanding, 8th North Stafford Regiment.

24th March, 1918.

At 8 a.m. the position held by the battalion was shelled continuously.

At 9 a.m. orders were received from the Division that the battalion was to be relieved immediately by the R. . W. Division, and at 9.20 a.m. an officer reported to me with same orders I had received, informing me that he had his battalion at BANCOURT and was ready to carry out the relief. I reported to O.C., 8th North Stafford Regiment and the relief was carried out by 10.30 a.m. On the way out of the position, the battalion did not return to Headquarters owing to the heavy shelling of the Valley in front of the Headquarters, but came out by the road South of BANCOURT and proceeded to REINCOURT where I halted and reported to the Brigade that the relief was complete and asked for orders, as the only orders I had received were from the Division.

While awaiting the orders the B.G.C., 154th Infantry Brigade, came up to me and gave me orders to take the battalion across the BAPAUME - PERONNE Road and act as a reserve to his Brigade.

At 12 noon the B.G.C. came up and issued orders to form a line in front of BEULENCOURT extending each side of the BAPAUME - PERONNE Road to cover the withdrawal of the 17th Division. The whole Battalion were in the line, in two lines - "A" and "B" Companies North of the Road, "C" and "D" Companies, South - the Front line in shell holes and the Support line in an old trench and in shell holes, the 6th Brigade on our right and the 6th Seaforth Highlanders on our left.

About 4.30 p.m. the 17th Division were reported
to be falling back but not fighting, and half an
hour after they came through the line on our left and
the troops of our line withdrew with them. Our left
flank was left in the air and "A" Company came back
in good order, having been under heavy machine gun
fire and fire from a field gun in LE TRANSLOY. At the
time they withdrew the enemy was within 250 yards of
them coming from the direction of VILLERS-AU-FLOS.
There were also enemy troops in a small wood on their
front and along the huts North of the Main road. In
the meantime "B" Company was under machine gun fire
from three guns but could not see the enemy advancing
owing to the huts on their half right front which was
where the enemy was assembling, but saw large forces
of the enemy in LE TRANSLOY and also a field gun
brought up which fired on our lines and on REULENCOURT.

"A" Company having withdrawn, "B" Company went,
when the enemy were within 400 yards in front of them
and only 200 yards on their right, among the huts.

O.C. "C" Company states as follows :-

"At about 5 p.m. I received a message from O.C. "B"
Company that the enemy were advancing up the main road
from LE TRANSLOY and to watch it. On receipt of this
I put another Lewis Gun on the main road (I had one
there before) and shortly after I saw the enemy coming
down the main road in fours about 800 to 1,000 yards
away. These two Lewis Guns fired about 30 drums which
held up the enemy on the road. Half an hour afterwards
I saw the enemy coming down the slope in front of LE
TRANSLOY and they were fired at and held up, and sent
up Very Lights to the artillery. I then went to my
right flank to find out what the situation was and
found a General and a Brigadier in a trench in which
was a red and white flag. I asked them what the
situation on the right was and the General said that
it was alright, and that he would hold on till 9 p.m.
Shortly after, the Brigadier came along and said that
he was outflanked as the enemy was coming down the
valley on our right, and that he was withdrawing. I
sent a message to O.C. "B" Company informing him of
this. After waiting till the messenger returned from
"B" Company I withdrew my company. The enemy was then
only on the outskirts of LE TRANSLOY on my front".

I had left my headquarters and was collecting
the men of this Division whom I saw retiring, and
formed a line with them in the water-pipe Trench 500
yards in rear of BEAULENCOURT and South of the main
road, but when my battalion withdrew this trench was
so crowded that I formed another line on the ridge
600 yards in rear, with the left flank well back
parallel to the road. By this time the general
retirement was stopped and I got in touch with O.C.
4th Seaforth Highlanders and O.C. 4th Gordon
Highlanders and they got their men together and I
reported the situation to Brigade. I extended the 4th
Seaforth Highlanders along the main road as the enemy
was showing lights on our flank the other side of the
road. About 7.30 p.m. orders were received from the
Brigade to proceed to LOUPART WOOD. The battalion
assembled at TILLOY WOOD and reached WARLENCOURT at
10.20 p.m. when our new position was explained.

The disposition was as follows :-
Our left flank was 200 yards South of LOUPART WOOD, next the 6th Seaforth Highlanders and ran South just behind the Sunken road to where it joined the 154th Infantry Brigade on the Sunken road leading to WARLENCOURT. "A", "C" & "D" Companies in front, "B" Company in Support, the whole in shell holes.
The night was quiet.

25th March, 1918.

Orders were received that the 19th Division were to withdraw through our front. Except for a slight shelling the morning was quiet and at mid-day the enemy could be seen on the skyline two miles away. About this time orders were received that the 62nd Division was on its way up to reinforce our line and that we must hold out till it arrived.
At 12.45 p.m. O.C. 7th Argyll & Sutherland Highlanders asked me if I could hang on and I informed him that there was nothing on my front to prevent my staying there. At 1 p.m. O.C. 7th Argyll & Sutherland Highlanders came to me and informed me that he must withdraw as the enemy were in great numbers on his right flank. I informed my right company - "A" Company - to try and keep in touch with 7th Argyll & Sutherland Highlanders, but they came back so quickly that he could not and withdrew.
"C" & "D" Companies remained in their positions for another quarter of an hour and engaged the enemy on their left front at about 600 yards, then they withdrew through "B" Company and suffered many casualties during this withdrawal. "B" Company remained till "C" & "D" Companies had gone across the ravine behind and then withdrew being engaged with the enemy who were in the sunken road on our front.
I tried to form a line with my battalion on the high ground East of IRLES and "B", "C" & "D" Companies got into position but the other troops would not remain, so the whole line came back to IRLES.
Ammunition was getting short at about 5 p.m. and shortly afterwards a general retirement took place to COLIN CAMPS. This battalion was engaged with the enemy at the time of the withdrawal. A mixed force, including "B" and some of "A" Company and four officers of this battalion, got in touch with the 62nd Division and held a line to the right of the railway by PUSIEUX till orders were received to withdraw at midnight.
When the 152nd Infantry Brigade got to SAILLY-AU-BOIS, there were only 2 officers and 120 men. This party bivouaced in FRONTVILLERS and got a hot meal at 4 a.m. from the Cookers.

26th March, 1918.

At 5 a.m. orders were received to put out outposts South of SAILLY-AU-BOIS, 6th Seaforth Highlanders on my right and 153rd Infantry Brigade on my left.
At 9 a.m. orders were received to withdraw in the formation in which we were, with the main party on the road SAILLY-AU-BOIS - BAYENCOURT - SOUASTRE, 500 yards from the village of SOUASTRE the battalion took up a line across the road, 4 platoons on the

right of the road and four platoons on the left, with the right flank well back covering the valley in front. At 1 p.m. the battalion was relieved by an Australian battalion, had a hot meal at SOUASTRE and moved to PAS where it bivouaced the night.

During these operations the men had undergone a severe strain -
(i) From the enemy's bombardment on the 21st March and subsequent fighting, and
(ii) From the exposure to cold nights without greatcoats or any adequate means of keeping warm which was unavoidable as their coats and packs were all left in the trenches on the 21st March, 1918. Owing to the severe cold at nights they got no real rest.

Owing to the excellent arrangements of the Staff Captain, a hot meal was provided on four days and on the 23rd March, besides a hot meal, this battalion got hot tea at night.

The absence of any artillery support was noticeable on the morning of the 21st March when masses of the enemy troops were seen to be assembling in LOUVERVAL WOOD all day and not a shell was fired at it. There were not many of our aeroplanes about the front line on the morning of the 21st March which may account for the artillery not taking advantage of some good targets.
On the night of the 22nd March there was much traffic on the BAPAUME - CAMBRAI Road which was not taken on by our artillery.
There was also a noticeable absence of artillery support in the operations of the 23rd 24th & 25th March.

The absence of any defensive line behind the BEAUMETZ - MORCHIES Line no doubt increased our casualties and added to the already great strain on the men by having to dig hurried positions wherever they were ordered under shell fire.

Our aeroplanes after the first day appeared to have complete command of our front.

A special feature during the retirement from IRLES to COLIN CAMPS when the troops were somewhat disorganised, was the escort formed by our aeroplanes who guarded the column the whole way and never gave an enemy aeroplane a chance of coming near the column as it withdrew.

Lewis Guns, when in good position and well manned, proved over and over again how important this weapon is in inflicting casualties on the enemy and holding them up.

The control of rifle fire is part of the training of men which requires special attention. A few instances of a good rifle section under fire control proved how important this is.

Rifle Grenades. None were used by this battalion after the 21st March. Owing to the enemy bombardment the supply on the 21st March was inadequate in the front and support lines as all the recesses were buried or blown up. The same applies to bombs but fresh supplies of these were sent up from the Intermediate Line.

                A A Duff
                              Major,
Commanding 6th Gordon Highlanders.

31st March, 1918.

1/6TH BATTALION, GORDON HIGHLANDERS.

1918.   Appendix.

March	FREMICOURT	
1st	Companies at the disposal of Company Commanders for inspection of Trench Kit, and preparing for the line. Battalion moved off from camp at 7.45 p.m., 100 yards interval between platoons. Guides were met at post 20 (J.10.a.3.3.) and the relief of the 4th Gordon Highlanders commenced and was completed at 12.30 a.m. The Battalion occupies the Brigade Centre Sector Left Sub. Sector; running from D.20.c.8.4. left to J.6.a.5.2. right. "D" Company LEFT front, "B" Company RIGHT front, "C" Company SUPPORT, and "A" Company RESERVE. Battalion Headquarters at J.10.b.0.7.	Reference Map- 57C:1/40,000 O.O.169

IN TRENCHES

2nd	Forenoon spent reconnoitring Front line and Defensive posts. Work of wiring Sunken Road, J.4.3.b.1.-J.5.c.0.3. arranged for when dark. 2 Officers and 100 men employed. Weather very cold with intermittent snow showers. 450 yards of wire put up in afternoon. The work of cleaning and repairing Front and Support lines went on all day. Enemy very quiet all day and night. Thickening front wire.
3rd	A dull morning and slight rain. Wiring of Sunken Road. Construction and improvement of fire bays in front and support lines. 800 yards of wiring done on Sunken Road and BOURSIES. The night passed quietly.
4th	Dull, damp, cold morning. Quiet night. Owing to the mist it was possible to wire the reserve line all day and 1100 yards were completed as well as part thickened by "C" Company. "D" Company thickened up wire opposite No.20 Post. A party was also working clearing the berm of FISH AVENUE and making fire-steps.
5th	Cold dull morning turned into a fine drying day. The wiring of the reserve line completed in the morning. Work on duckboards in support line. Revetting firesteps in front line and support line.

1918.   Appendix.

March

5th (Ctd).
Digging and enlarging Post 21 also improving Posts 18 & 19. Quiet night.

6th
Frost at night, fine day but hazy and visibility bad. Usual work on trenches, repairing and making firesteps. Enlarging Post 21 and digging firesteps between Posts 19 & 20. Wiring and improving trenches. Battalion to be relieved to-morrow by the 6th Seaforth Highlanders.

7th
The usual work. General ALEXANDER of the U.S. Army was taken round our trenches and shown everything this morning. Owing to a haze the relief took place in daylight between 4 p.m. and 6 p.m. We had two casualties coming out and it was very lucky we had not more as an eight inch shell burst on the CAMBRAI - BAPAUME Road amongst a section and only two men were wounded. The Battalion is in huts at O'SHEA CAMP in Brigade Reserve.   O.O.170

O'SHEA CAMP

8th
O'SHEA CAMP. Cleaning up and improving camp. Company Commanders reconnoitring routes and positions in Reserve Line.

9th
Battalion at Baths all day.

10th
Church Parade.

11th
"A" & "C" Companies inspected by Commanding Officer. All Respirators inspected. Reconnoitring Front Line.

12th
All companies inspected by Commanding Officer. Officers reconnoitring line.

13th
The Battalion moved off to the line, the first Company moving off at 12.30 p.m 300 yards between Sections. The Battalion took over Centre Battalion Sector from 5th Seaforth Highlanders. "A" Company - Front Line, "C" Company - Support, "B" Company - Intermediate and "D" Company - Reserve Line.   O.O.171

14th
All available men in Support and Intermediate Lines working 8 hours per day on wiring and general trench repair.

15th
Weather very fine. Same work as yesterday. Party of 75 men carrying 60 lb. bombs to No Man's Land.

1918.   Appendix.

March

16th   Work as above, enemy quiet.

17th   Work as above, enemy quiet.

18th   Work as above. Enemy registering
        on batteries and DOIGNIES and
        DOIGNIES - DEMICOURT Road.

        IN TRENCHES

19th   Inter-Company relief. "C" Company
        relieved "A" Company in Front
        Line. "B" Company relieved "C"   O.O.172
        Company. "A" Company came back to
        Intermediate Line. Working parties
        suspended on account of relief.

20th   During day men rested. At night
        all available men on working
        parties digging new reserve line
        from J.5.c.1.0. to BOURSIES -
        DOIGNIES Road. Battalion worked
        in two shifts. First from 7.15 p.m.
        to 11.30 p.m., second 11.45 p.m.
        to 3 a.m. Trench completed.

21st   For report on operations from
to   21st to 26th March, 1918 see
26th   Appendix attached hereto.

        NEUVILLETTE

27th   The Battalion were to embus from
        PAS to NEUVILLETTE, but owing to
        the uncertainty of the arrival of
        the buses we were given the option
        of marching about 8 miles which we
        did. Starting at 10.45 a.m. having
        dinners en route from the Cookers
        at POMMERA and arriving at
        NEUVILLETTE at 4.30 p.m. where the
        Battalion was billetted in comfortable
        billets. Indents for kit already
        gone in.

28th   The Battalion resting and cleaning up.
        Some of the fighting equipment
        indented for arrived.

        NEUVILLETTE - LABEUVRIERE

29th   Orders were received to march to
        FREVENT and then to entrain for the
        LILLERS area at 1 p.m. The Battalion   O.O.173
        left at 10.15 a.m. Cookers were   O.O.174
        sent on and the men had their
        dinners in a field near the
        station. While resting after
        their dinners the King's car was
        seen coming along the road and
        the Battalion received him with
        tremendous cheering. Whereupon
        His Majesty stopped his car and
        spoke to several officers and

1918.   Appendix.

March

29th   N.C.Os. Then the Battalion was
(Ctd). marched past the King and His
        Majesty expressed his admiration for
        the appearance of the Battalion and
        his pleasure at having seen them.
        The train left FREVENT at 3.30 p.m.
        and arrived at LAPUGNOY at 6 p.m.
        The Battalion was billetted at
        LABEUVRIERE quite close to the
        Station in good billets.

        LABEUVRIERE

30th   Battalion resting at LABEUVRIERE.

31st   Battalion cleaning up. More equipment
        arrived from the Ordnance.

        HONOURS & AWARDS
            NIL.
                                            Officers   O.R.
        Strength at end of last month   42   1012
        ADD:-   Off. O.R.
        Drafts ... ...   -   46
        Casuals... ... ...   -   15
        Officers joined during month   2 - 2   61
                                                 44   1073
        DEDUCT:-
        Evacuations   98
        To United Kingdom for Commission -   2
        To Base - Tradesmen   ...   -   2
        To U.K. - Officers' Substitution 2   -
                        Scheme.
        To 51st (S) Battn. M.G.C.   -   9
        Casualties :-
        Killed   )   2   35
        Wounded   ) as Per   11   159
        Unaccounted For   ) Appendix   3   74
        Died of Wounds   )   - 6   18   385

        Strength at end of this month ...   26   688

                        A A DUFF
                                Major
                    Commanding 6th Gordon Highlanders.

ACCOUNT OF OPERATIONS commencing near
BOURSIES on 21st March, 1918, and
lasting till 26th March, 1918.

21st March, 1918.

4.45 a.m. Intense bombardment of British lines, Front, Support, and Intermediate lines all being included. Barrage consisted of 8", 5.9" and gas shells.

The QUARRY was barraged and a large number of gas shells fell in and around it.

9.15 a.m. Enemy seen bombing along STURGEON SUPPORT Trench from direction of BOURSIES. What men were left in Front line were withdrawn to Support line and a block was formed in the trench and the enemy held up.

A platoon from the QUARRY had been moved up and manned STURGEON AVENUE between Sunk Road and STURGEON SUPPORT.

10.15 a.m. The troops in STURGEON SUPPORT were driven out. Enemy were now in STURGEON AVENUE and tried to bomb down towards BOURSIES - CRUCIFIX Road. A block was made in STURGEON AVENUE and enemy held up.

11 a.m. Bombs ran short and block was forced down STURGEON AVENUE a short distance.

11.30 a.m. Enemy in great numbers seen coming from BOURSIES and trying to get down BOURSIES - DOIGNIES Road. Three Lewis Guns and all rifles in STURGEON AVENUE opened fire on them inflicting many casualties. The garrison by this time was forced down STURGEON AVENUE some eighty yards south of BOURSIES - CRUCIFIX Road and a block established there. More bombs and rifle grenades arrived from Battalion Headquarters and enemy were again held up for about an hour.

1.30 p.m. Owing to increasing enemy pressure from front and left flank the block in STURGEON had again to fall back about seventy yards below the QUARRY. This position was held till orders were received to withdraw at 1.30 a.m. on 22nd March, 1918.

The platoon at J.5.c.1.0. on CAMBRAI Road were nearly all taken prisoners. They held their position till nearly surrounded and then only the officer and four men got away down the BOURSIES - DOIGNIES Road to the Intermediate Line.

"A" Company and two platoons of "D" Company in the Intermediate Line were heavily shelled and gassed. When enemy were seen coming out of BOURSIES they were ordered to counter-attack, but, owing to the heavy machine gun fire from the hedge in front of the Reserve line the attack was held up. After this "A" Company lost touch on their left flank and withdrew and formed a defensive flank South of DOIGNIES which was shortly afterwards occupied by the enemy. This line was held till 1.30 a.m.

The remaining two platoons of "D" Company who were in reserve at LEBUCQUIERE held a part of the BEAUMETZ - MORCHIES line South of the BAPAUME - CAMBRAI Road till 2 a.m. on the 23rd March, 1918.

22nd March, 1918.

At 1.30 a.m. the battalion was ordered to take up a position along the plank Road in J.19. and D.20.c. and remained there till 1.30 p.m. when orders were received to hold a line on the North side of the BAPAUME - CAMBRAI Road covering BEUGNY.

At 3 p.m. orders were received to proceed to MIDDLESEX CAMP where the battalion had a hot meal.

At 5.30 p.m. the battalion was ordered to form a line along the railway 1500 yards North of FREMICOURT facing BEUGNATRE.

23rd March, 1918.

At 1 a.m. the battalion was withdrawn to MIDDLESEX CAMP when a hot meal was provided for the men and where Echelon B joined the battalion.

At 12 noon orders were received to take up a position on a line 200 yards North and South of MILL CROSS facing LEBUCQUIERE; the line North of MILL CROSS was astride the FREMICOURT - LEBUCQUIERE Road. This line was 600 yards from the Green line. The orders were to reinforce Green line if necessary and hold our line. The line was held in section posts - "B" and "C" Companies in Front line, "A" and "D" Companies in support. This position was intermittently shelled during the afternoon and evening.

At 4 p.m. orders were received that the battalion was attached to the 56th Brigade and under orders of the Officer Commanding, 8th North Stafford Regiment.

24th March, 1918.

At 8 a.m. the position held by the battalion was shelled continuously.

At 9 a.m. orders were received from the Division that the battalion was to be relieved immediately by the R. . W. Division, and at 9.20 a.m. an officer reported to me with same orders I had received, informing me that he had his battalion at BANCOURT and was ready to carry out the relief. I reported to O.C., 8th North Stafford Regiment and the relief was carried out by 10.30 a.m. On the way out of the position, the battalion did not return to Headquarters owing to the heavy shelling of the Valley in front of the Headquarters, but came out by the road South of BANCOURT and proceeded to REINCOURT where I halted and reported to the Brigade that the relief was complete and asked for orders, as the only orders I had received were from the Division.

While awaiting the orders the B.G.C., 154th Infantry Brigade, came up to me and gave me orders to take the battalion across the BAPAUME - PERONNE Road and act as a reserve to his Brigade.

At 12 noon the B.G.C. came up and issued orders to form a line in front of BEULENCOURT extending each side of the BAPAUME - PERONNE Road to cover the withdrawal of the 17th Division. The whole Battalion were in the line, in two lines - "A" and "B" Companies North of the Road, "C" and "D" Companies, South - the Front line in shell holes and the Support line in an old trench and in shell holes, the 6th Brigade on our right and the 6th Seaforth Highlanders on our left.

About 4.30 p.m. the 17th Division were reported to be falling back but not fighting, and half an hour after they came through the line on our left and the troops of our line withdrew with them. Our left flank was left in the air and "A" Company came back in good order, having been under heavy machine gun fire and fire from a field gun in LE TRANSLOY. At the time they withdrew the enemy was within 250 yards of them coming from the direction of VILLERS-AU-FLOS. There were also enemy troops in a small wood on their front and along the huts North of the Main road. In the meantime "B" Company was under machine gun fire from three guns but could not see the enemy advancing owing to the huts on their half right front which was where the enemy was assembling, but saw large forces of the enemy in LE TRANSLOY and also a field gun brought up which fired on our lines and on REULENCOURT.

"A" Company having withdrawn, "B" Company went, when the enemy were within 400 yards in front of them and only 200 yards on their right, among the huts.

O.C. "C" Company states as follows :-

"At about 5 p.m. I received a message from O.C. "B" Company that the enemy were advancing up the main road from LE TRANSLOY and to watch it. On receipt of this I put another Lewis Gun on the main road (I had one there before) and shortly after I saw the enemy coming down the main road in fours about 800 to 1,000 yards away. These two Lewis Guns fired about 30 drums which held up the enemy on the road. Half an hour afterwards I saw the enemy coming down the slope in front of LE TRANSLOY and they were fired at and held up, and sent up Very Lights to the artillery. I then went to my right flank to find out what the situation was and found a General and a Brigadier in a trench in which was a red and white flag. I asked them what the situation on the right was and the General said that it was alright, and that he would hold on till 9 p.m. Shortly after, the Brigadier came along and said that he was outflanked as the enemy was coming down the valley on our right, and that he was withdrawing. I sent a message to O.C. "B" Company informing him of this. After waiting till the messenger returned from "B" Company I withdrew my company. The enemy was then only on the outskirts of LE TRANSLOY on my front".

I had left my headquarters and was collecting the men of this Division whom I saw retiring, and formed a line with them in the water-pipe Trench 500 yards in rear of BEAULENCOURT and South of the main road, but when my battalion withdrew this trench was so crowded that I formed another line on the ridge 600 yards in rear, with the left flank well back parallel to the road. By this time the general retirement was stopped and I got in touch with O.C. 4th Seaforth Highlanders and O.C. 4th Gordon Highlanders and they got their men together and I reported the situation to Brigade. I extended the 4th Seaforth Highlanders along the main road as the enemy was showing lights on our flank the other side of the road. About 7.30 p.m. orders were received from the Brigade to proceed to LOUPART WOOD. The battalion assembled at TILLOY WOOD and reached WARLENCOURT at 10.20 p.m. when our new position was explained.

The disposition was as follows :-
Our left flank was 200 yards South of LOUPART WOOD, next the 6th Seaforth Highlanders and ran South just behind the Sunken road to where it joined the 154th Infantry Brigade on the Sunken road leading to WARLENCOURT. "A", "C" & "D" Companies in front, "B" Company in Support, the whole in shell holes.

The night was quiet.

25th March, 1918.

Orders were received that the 19th Division were to withdraw through our front. Except for a slight shelling the morning was quiet and at mid-day the enemy could be seen on the skyline two miles away. About this time orders were received that the 62nd Division was on its way up to reinforce our line and that we must hold out till it arrived.

At 12.45 p.m. O.C. 7th Argyll & Sutherland Highlanders asked me if I could hang on and I informed him that there was nothing on my front to prevent my staying there. At 1 p.m. O.C. 7th Argyll & Sutherland Highlanders came to me and informed me that he must withdraw as the enemy were in great numbers on his right flank. I informed my right company - "A" Company - to try and keep in touch with 7th Argyll & Sutherland Highlanders, but they came back so quickly that he could not and withdrew.

"C" & "D" Companies remained in their positions for another quarter of an hour and engaged the enemy on their left front at about 600 yards, then they withdrew through "B" Company and suffered many casualties during this withdrawal. "B" Company remained till "C" & "D" Companies had gone across the ravine behind and then withdrew being engaged with the enemy who were in the sunken road on our front.

I tried to form a line with my battalion on the high ground East of IRLES and "B", "C" & "D" Companies got into position but the other troops would not remain, so the whole line came back to IRLES.

Ammunition was getting short at about 5 p.m. and shortly afterwards a general retirement took place to COLIN CAMPS. This battalion was engaged with the enemy at the time of the withdrawal. A mixed force, including "B" and some of "A" Company and four officers of this battalion, got in touch with the 62nd Division and held a line to the right of the railway by PUSIEUX till orders were received to withdraw at midnight.

When the 152nd Infantry Brigade got to SAILLY-AU-BOIS, there were only 2 officers and 120 men. This party bivouaced in FRONTVILLERS and got a hot meal at 4 a.m. from the Cookers.

26th March, 1918.

At 5 a.m. orders were received to put out outposts South of SAILLY-AU-BOIS, 6th Seaforth Highlanders on my right and 153rd Infantry Brigade on my left.

At 9 a.m. orders were received to withdraw in the formation in which we were, with the main party on the road SAILLY-AU-BOIS - BAYENCOURT - SOUASTRE, 500 yards from the village of SOUASTRE the battalion took up a line across the road, 4 platoons on the

right of the road and four platoons on the left,
with the right flank well back covering the valley
in front.   At 1 p.m. the battalion was relieved by
an Australian battalion, had a hot meal at SOUASTRE
and moved to PAS where it bivouaced the night.

During these operations the men had
undergone a severe strain -
(i) From the enemy's bombardment on the 21st March
and subsequent fighting, and
(ii) From the exposure to cold nights without
greatcoats or any adequate means of keeping
warm which was unavoidable as their coats
and packs were all left in the trenches on
the 21st March, 1918. Owing to the severe
cold at nights they got no real rest.

Owing to the excellent arrangements of the
Staff Captain, a hot meal was provided on four days
and on the 23rd March, besides a hot meal, this
battalion got hot tea at night.

The absence of any artillery support was
noticeable on the morning of the 21st March when
masses of the enemy troops were seen to be assembling
in LOUVERVAL WOOD all day and not a shell was fired
at it. There were not many of our aeroplanes about
the front line on the morning of the 21st March which
may account for the artillery not taking advantage
of some good targets.
On the night of the 22nd March there was much
traffic on the BAPAUME - CAMBRAI Road which was not
taken on by our artillery.
There was also a noticeable absence of
artillery support in the operations of the 23rd
24th & 25th March.

The absence of any defensive line behind the
BEAUMETZ - MORCHIES Line no doubt increased our
casualties and added to the already great strain on
the men by having to dig hurried positions wherever
they were ordered under shell fire.

Our aeroplanes after the first day appeared to
have complete command of our front.

A special feature during the retirement from
IRLES to COLIN CAMPS when the troops were somewhat
disorganised, was the escort formed by our aeroplanes
who guarded the column the whole way and never gave
an enemy aeroplane a chance of coming near the column
as it withdrew.

Lewis Guns, when in good position and well
manned, proved over and over again how important this
weapon is in inflicting casualties on the enemy
and holding them up.

The control of rifle fire is part of the training of men which requires special attention. A few instances of a good rifle section under fire control proved how important this is.

Rifle Grenades. None were used by this battalion after the 21st March. Owing to the enemy bombardment the supply on the 21st March was inadequate in the front and support lines as all the recesses were buried or blown up. The same applies to bombs but fresh supplies of these were sent up from the Intermediate Line.

                A A Duff
                            Major,
    Commanding 6th Gordon Highlanders.

31st March, 1918.

1/6TH BATTALION, GORDON HIGHLANDERS.

1918.   Appendix.

March   FREMICOURT

1st   Companies at the disposal of   Reference
             Company Commanders for   Map
             inspection of Trench Kit,   57C;1/40,000
             and preparing for the line.   O.O.169
             Battalion moved off from camp
             at 7.45 p.m., 100 yards interval
             between platoons. Guides were
             met at post 20 (J.10.a.3.3.)
             and the relief of the 4th
             Gordon Highlanders commenced
             and was completed at 12.30 a.m.
             The Battalion occupies the
             Brigade Centre Sector Left Sub.
             Sector, running from
             D.20.c.8.4. left to J.6.a.5.2.
             right. "D" Company LEFT front,
             "B" Company RIGHT front, "C"
             Company SUPPORT, and "A" Company
             RESERVE. Battalion Headquarters
             at J.10.b.0.7.

             IN TRENCHES

2nd   Forenoon spent reconnoitring Front
             line and Defensive posts. Work
             of wiring Sunken Road, J.4.3.b.1. -
             J.5.c.0.3. arranged for when dark.
             2 Officers and 100 men employed.
             Weather very cold with intermittent
             snow showers. 450 yards of wire
             put up in afternoon. The work of
             cleaning and repairing Front and
             Support lines went on all day.
             Enemy very quiet all day and
             night. Thickening front wire.

3rd   A dull morning and slight rain.
             Wiring of Sunken Road. Construction
             and improvement of fire bays in
             front and support lines. 800 yards
             of wiring done on Sunken Road
             and BOURSIES. The night passed
             quietly.

4th   Dull, damp, cold morning. Quiet
             night. Owing to the mist
             it was possible to wire the
             reserve line all day and 1100
             yards were completed as well
             as part thickened by "C" Company.
             "D" Company thickened up wire
             opposite No.20 Post. A party
             was also working clearing the
             berm of FISH AVENUE and making
             fire-steps.

5th   Cold dull morning turned into a
             fine drying day. The wiring of
             the reserve line completed in the
             morning. Work on duckboards in
             support line. Revetting firesteps
             in front line and support line.

1918.   Appendix.

March

5th
(Ctd).   Digging and enlarging Post 21
          also improving Posts 18 & 19.
          Quiet night.

6th   Frost at night, fine day but hazy
          and visibility bad. Usual work on
          trenches, repairing and making
          firesteps. Enlarging Post 21
          and digging firesteps between
          Posts 19 & 20. Wiring and
          improving trenches. Battalion
          to be relieved to-morrow by the 6th
          Seaforth Highlanders.

7th   The usual work. General ALEXANDER
          of the U.S. Army was taken round
          our trenches and shown everything
          this morning. Owing to a haze the   O.O.170
          relief took place in daylight
          between 4 p.m. and 6 p.m. We had
          two casualties coming out and it
          was very lucky we had not more
          as an eight inch shell burst on
          the CAMBRAI - BAPAUME Road amongst
          a section and only two men were
          wounded. The Battalion is in huts
          at O'SHEA CAMP in Brigade Reserve.

          O'SHEA CAMP

8th   O'SHEA CAMP. Cleaning up and
          improving camp. Company Commanders
          reconnoitring routes and positions
          in Reserve Line.

9th   Battalion at Baths all day.

10th   Church Parade.

11th   "A" & "C" Companies inspected by
          Commanding Officer. All Respirators
          inspected. Reconnoitring Front Line.

12th   All companies inspected by Commanding
          Officer. Officers reconnoitring
          line.

13th   The Battalion moved off to the line,
          the first Company moving off at   O.O.171
          12.30 p.m 300 yards between Sections.
          The Battalion took over Centre
          Battalion Sector from 5th Seaforth
          Highlanders. "A" Company - Front
          Line, "C" Company - Support,
          "B" Company - Intermediate and
          "D" Company - Reserve Line.

14th   All available men in Support and
          Intermediate Lines working 8 hours
          per day on wiring and general trench
          repair.

15th   Weather very fine. Same work as
          yesterday. Party of 75 men carrying
          50 lb. bombs to No Man's Land.

1918.   Appendix

March

16th   Work as above, enemy quiet.

17th   Work as above, enemy quiet.

18th   Work as above. Enemy registering
        on batteries and DOIGNIES and
        DOIGNIES - DEMICOURT Road.

        IN TRENCHES

19th   Inter-Company relief. "C" Company
        relieved "A" Company in Front
        Line. "B" Company relieved "C"   O.O.172
        Company. "A" Company came back to
        Intermediate Line. Working parties
        suspended on account of relief.

20th   During day men rested. At night
        all available men on working
        parties digging new reserve line
        from J.5.c.1.0. to BOURSIES -
        DOIGNIES Road. Battalion worked
        in two shifts. First from 7.15 p.m.
        to 11.30 p.m., second 11.45 p.m.
        to 3 a.m. Trench completed.

21st   For report on operations from
to   21st to 26th March, 1918 see
26th   Appendix attached hereto.

        NEUVILLETTE

27th   The Battalion were to embus from
        PAS to NEUVILLETTE, but owing to
        the uncertainty of the arrival of
        the buses we were given the option
        of marching about 8 miles which we
        did. Starting at 10.45 a.m. having
        dinners en route from the Cookers
        at POMMERA and arriving at
        NEUVILLETTE at 4.30 p.m. where the
        Battalion was billetted in comfortable
        billets. Indents for kit already
        gone in.

28th   The Battalion resting and cleaning up.
        Some of the fighting equipment
        indented for arrived.

        NEUVILLETTE - LABEUVRIERE

29th   Orders were received to march to
        FREVENT and then to entrain for the
        LILLERS area at 1 p.m. The Battalion   O.O.173
        left at 10.15 a.m. Cookers were   O.O.174
        sent on and the men had their
        dinners in a field near the
        station. While resting after
        their dinners the King's car was
        seen coming along the road and
        the Battalion received him with
        tremendous cheering. Whereupon
        His Majesty stopped his car and
        spoke to several officers and

1918.   Appendix.

March

29th   N.C.Os. Then the Battalion was
(Ctd).   marched past the King and His
         Majesty expressed his admiration for
         the appearance of the Battalion and
         his pleasure at having seen them.
         The train left FREVENT at 3.30 p.m.
         and arrived at LAPUGNOY at 6 p.m.
         The Battalion was billetted at
         LABEUVRIERE quite close to the
         Station in good billets.

         LABEUVRIERE

30th   Battalion resting at LABEUVRIERE.

31st   Battalion cleaning up. More equipment
         arrived from the Ordnance.
         HONOURS & AWARDS
              NIL.
                                              Officers O.R.
         Strength at end of last month   42   1012
         ADD:-   Off. O.R.
         Drafts ... ...   -   46
         Casuals... ... ...   -   15
         Officers joined during month   2   -   2   61
                                                              44   1073
         DEDUCT:-
         Evacuations   98
         To United Kingdom for Commission   -   2
         To Base - Tradesmen   ...   -   2
         To U.K. - Officers' Substitution   2   -
                         Scheme.
         To 51st (S) Battn. M.G.C.   -   9
         Casualties :-
         Killed   )   2   35
         Wounded   ) as Per   11   159
         Unaccounted For) Appendix   3   74
         Died of Wounds)   -   6   18   385

         Strength at end of this month ...   26   688

                              A A DUFF
                                        Major
                         Commanding 6th Gordon Highlanders.

ACCOUNT OF OPERATIONS commencing near
BOURSIES on 21st March, 1918, and
lasting till 26th March, 1918.

21st March, 1918.

4.45 a.m. Intense bombardment of British lines, Front, Support, and Intermediate lines all being included. Barrage consisted of 8", 5.9" and gas shells.

The QUARRY was barraged and a large number of gas shells fell in and around it.

9.15 a.m. Enemy seen bombing along STURGEON SUPPORT Trench from direction of BOURSIES. What men were left in Front line were withdrawn to Support line and a block was formed in the trench and the enemy held up.

A platoon from the QUARRY had been moved up and manned STURGEON AVENUE between Sunk Road and STURGEON SUPPORT.

10.15 a.m. The troops in STURGEON SUPPORT were driven out. Enemy were now in STURGEON AVENUE and tried to bomb down towards BOURSIES - CRUCIFIX Road. A block was made in STURGEON AVENUE and enemy held up.

11 a.m. Bombs ran short and block was forced down STURGEON AVENUE a short distance.

11.30 a.m. Enemy in great numbers seen coming from BOURSIES and trying to get down BOURSIES - DOIGNIES Road. Three Lewis Guns and all rifles in STURGEON AVENUE opened fire on them inflicting many casualties. The garrison by this time was forced down STURGEON AVENUE some eighty yards south of BOURSIES - CRUCIFIX Road and a block established there. More bombs and rifle grenades arrived from Battalion Headquarters and enemy were again held up for about an hour.

1.30 p.m. Owing to increasing enemy pressure from front and left flank the block in STURGEON had again to fall back about seventy yards below the QUARRY. This position was held till orders were received to withdraw at 1.30 a.m. on 22nd March, 1918.

The platoon at J.5.c.1.0. on CAMBRAI Road were nearly all taken prisoners. They held their position till nearly surrounded and then only the officer and four men got away down the BOURSIES - DOIGNIES Road to the Intermediate Line.

"A" Company and two platoons of "D" Company in the Intermediate Line were heavily shelled and gassed. When enemy were seen coming out of BOURSIES they were ordered to counter-attack, but, owing to the heavy machine gun fire from the hedge in front of the Reserve line the attack was held up. After this "A" Company lost touch on their left flank and withdrew and formed a defensive flank South of DOIGNIES which was shortly afterwards occupied by the enemy. This line was held till 1.30 a.m.

The remaining two platoons of "D" Company who were in reserve at LEBUCQUIERE held a part of the BEAUMETZ - MORCHIES line South of the BAPAUME - CAMBRAI Road till 2 a.m. on the 23rd March, 1918.

22nd March, 1918.

At 1.30 a.m. the battalion was ordered to take up a position along the plank Road in J.19. and D.20.c. and remained there till 1.30 p.m. when orders were received to hold a line on the North side of the BAPAUME - CAMBRAI Road covering BEUGNY.

At 3 p.m. orders were received to proceed to MIDDLESEX CAMP where the battalion had a hot meal.

At 5.30 p.m. the battalion was ordered to form a line along the railway 1500 yards North of FREMICOURT facing BEUGNATRE.

23rd March, 1918.

At 1 a.m. the battalion was withdrawn to MIDDLESEX CAMP when a hot meal was provided for the men and where Echelon B joined the battalion.

At 12 noon orders were received to take up a position on a line 200 yards North and South of MILL CROSS facing LEBUCQUIERE; the line North of MILL CROSS was astride the FREMICOURT - LEBUCQUIERE Road. This line was 500 yards from the Green line. The orders were to reinforce Green line if necessary and hold our line. The line was held in section posts- "B" and "C" Companies in Front line, "A" and "D" Companies in support. This position was intermittently shelled during the afternoon and evening.

At 4 p.m. orders were received that the battalion was attached to the 56th Brigade and under orders of the Officer Commanding, 8th North Stafford Regiment.

24th March, 1918.

At 8 a.m. the position held by the battalion was shelled continuously.

At 9 a.m. orders were received from the Division that the battalion was to be relieved immediately by the R. . W. Division, and at 9.20 a.m. an officer reported to me with same orders I had received, informing me that he had his battalion at BANCOURT and was ready to carry out the relief. I reported to O.C., 8th North Stafford Regiment and the relief was carried out by 10.30 a.m. On the way out of the position, the battalion did not return to Headquarters owing to the heavy shelling of the Valley in front of the Headquarters, but came out by the road South of BANCOURT and proceeded to REINCOURT where I halted and reported to the Brigade that the relief was complete and asked for orders, as the only orders I had received were from the Division.

While awaiting the orders the B.G.C., 154th Infantry Brigade, came up to me and gave me orders to take the battalion across the BAPAUME - PERONNE Road and act as a reserve to his Brigade.

At 12 noon the B.G.C. came up and issued orders to form a line in front of BEULENCOURT extending each side of the BAPAUME - PERONNE Road to cover the withdrawal of the 17th Division. The whole Battalion were in the line, in two lines - "A" and "B" Companies North of the Road, "C" and "D" Companies, South - the Front line in shell holes and the Support line in an old trench and in shell holes, the 6th Brigade on our right and the 6th Seaforth Highlanders on our left.

About 4.30 p.m. the 17th Division were reported to be falling back but not fighting, and half an hour after they came through the line on our left and the troops of our line withdrew with them. Our left flank was left in the air and "A" Company came back in good order, having been under heavy machine gun fire and fire from a field gun in LE TRANSLOY. At the time they withdrew the enemy was within 250 yards of them coming from the direction of VILLERS-AU-FLOS. There were also enemy troops in a small wood on their front and along the huts North of the Main road. In the meantime "B" Company was under machine gun fire from three guns but could not see the enemy advancing owing to the huts on their half right front which was where the enemy was assembling, but saw large forces of the enemy in LE TRANSLOY and also a field gun brought up which fired on our lines and on BEULENCOURT.

"A" Company having withdrawn, "B" Company went, when the enemy were within 400 yards in front of them and only 200 yards on their right, among the huts.

O.C. "C" Company states as follows :-

"At about 5 p.m. I received a message from O.C. "B" Company that the enemy were advancing up the main road from LE TRANSLOY and to watch it. On receipt of this I put another Lewis Gun on the main road (I had one there before) and shortly after I saw the enemy coming down the main road in fours about 800 to 1,000 yards away. These two Lewis Guns fired about 30 drums which held up the enemy on the road. Half an hour afterwards I saw the enemy coming down the slope in front of LE TRANSLOY and they were fired at and held up, and sent up Very Lights to the artillery. I then went to my right flank to find out what the situation was and found a General and a Brigadier in a trench in which was a red and white flag. I asked them what the situation on the right was and the General said that it was alright, and that he would hold on till 9 p.m. Shortly after, the Brigadier came along and said that he was outflanked as the enemy was coming down the valley on our right, and that he was withdrawing. I sent a message to O.C. "B" Company informing him of this. After waiting till the messenger returned from "B" Company I withdrew my company. The enemy was then only on the outskirts of LE TRANSLOY on my front".

I had left my headquarters and was collecting the men of this Division whom I saw retiring, and formed a line with them in the water-pipe Trench 500 yards in rear of BEAULENCOURT and South of the main road, but when my battalion withdrew this trench was so crowded that I formed another line on the ridge 600 yards in rear, with the left flank well back parallel to the road. By this time the general retirement was stopped and I got in touch with O.C. 4th Seaforth Highlanders and O.C. 4th Gordon Highlanders and they got their men together and I reported the situation to Brigade. I extended the 4th Seaforth Highlanders along the main road as the enemy was showing lights on our flank the other side of the road. About 7.30 p.m. orders were received from the Brigade to proceed to LOUPART WOOD. The battalion assembled at TILLOY WOOD and reached WARLENCOURT at 10.20 p.m. when our new position was explained.

The disposition was as follows :-
Our left flank was 200 yards South of LOUPART WOOD, next the 6th Seaforth Highlanders and ran South just behind the Sunken road to where it joined the 154th Infantry Brigade on the Sunken road leading to WARLENCOURT. "A", "C" & "D" Companies in front, "B" Company in Support, the whole in shell holes.
The night was quiet.

25th March, 1918.

Orders were received that the 19th Division were to withdraw through our front. Except for a slight shelling the morning was quiet and at mid-day the enemy could be seen on the skyline two miles away. About this time orders were received that the 62nd Division was on its way up to reinforce our line and that we must hold out till it arrived.

At 12.45 p.m. O.C. 7th Argyll & Sutherland Highlanders asked me if I could hang on and I informed him that there was nothing on my front to prevent my staying there. At 1 p.m. O.C. 7th Argyll & Sutherland Highlanders came to me and informed me that he must withdraw as the enemy were in great numbers on his right flank. I informed my right company - "A" Company - to try and keep in touch with 7th Argyll & Sutherland Highlanders, but they came back so quickly that he could not and withdrew.

"C" & "D" Companies remained in their positions for another quarter of an hour and engaged the enemy on their left front at about 600 yards, then they withdrew through "B" Company and suffered many casualties during this withdrawal. "B" Company remained till "C" & "D" Companies had gone across the ravine behind and then withdrew being engaged with the enemy who were in the sunken road on our front.

I tried to form a line with my battalion on the high ground East of IRLES and "B", "C" & "D" Companies got into position but the other troops would not remain, so the whole line came back to IRLES.

Ammunition was getting short at about 5 p.m. and shortly afterwards a general retirement took place to COLIN CAMPS. This battalion was engaged with the enemy at the time of the withdrawal. A mixed force, including "B" and some of "A" Company and four officers of this battalion, got in touch with the 62nd Division and held a line to the right of the railway by PUSIEUX till orders were received to withdraw at midnight.

When the 152nd Infantry Brigade got to SAILLY-AU-BOIS, there were only 2 officers and 120 men. This party bivouaced in FRONTVILLERS and got a hot meal at 4 a.m. from the Cookers.

26th March, 1918.

At 5 a.m. orders were received to put out outposts South of SAILLY-AU-BOIS, 6th Seaforth Highlanders on my right and 152rd Infantry Brigade on my left.

At 9 a.m. orders were received to withdraw in the formation in which we were, with the main party on the road SAILLY-AU-BOIS - BAYENCOURT - SOUASTRE. 500 yards from the village of SOUASTRE the battalion took up a line across the road, 4 platoons on the right of the road and four platoons on the left, with the right flank well back covering the valley in front. At 1 p.m. the battalion was relieved by an Australian battalion, had a hot meal at SOUASTRE and moved to PAS where it bivouaced the night.

During these operations the men had undergone a severe strain -
(i) From the enemy's bombardment on the 21st March and subsequent fighting, and
(ii) From the exposure to cold nights without greatcoats or any adequate means of keeping warm which was unavoidable as their coats and packs were all left in the trenches on the 21st March, 1918. Owing to the severe cold at nights they got no real rest.

Owing to the excellent arrangements of the Staff Captain, a hot meal was provided on four days and on the 23rd March, besides a hot meal, this battalion got hot tea at night.

The absence of any artillery support was noticeable on the morning of the 21st March when masses of the enemy troops were seen to be assembling in LOUVERVAL WOOD all day and not a shell was fired at it. There were not many of our aeroplanes about the front line on the morning of the 21st March which may account for the artillery not taking advantage of some good targets.
On the night of the 22nd March there was much traffic on the BAPAUME - CAMBRAI Road which was not taken on by our artillery.
There was also a noticeable absence of artillery support in the operations of the 23rd 24th & 25th March.

The absence of any defensive line behind the BEAUMETZ - MORCHIES Line no doubt increased our casualties and added to the already great strain on the men by having to dig hurried positions wherever they were ordered under shell fire.

Our aeroplanes after the first day appeared to have complete command of our front.

A special feature during the retirement from IRLES to COLIN CAMPS when the troops were somewhat disorganised, was the escort formed by our aeroplanes who guarded the column the whole way and never gave an enemy aeroplane a chance of coming near the column as it withdrew.

Lewis Guns, when in good position and well manned, proved over and over again how important this weapon is in inflicting casualties on the enemy and holding them up.

The control of rifle fire is part of the training of men which requires special attention. A few instances of a good rifle section under fire control proved how important this is.

Rifle Grenades. None were used by this battalion after the 21st March. Owing to the enemy bombardment the supply on the 21st March was inadequate in the front and support lines as all the recesses were buried or blown up. The same applies to bombs but fresh supplies of these were sent up from the Intermediate Line.

            A A Duff
                    Major,
Commanding 6th Gordon Highlanders.

31st March, 1918.

CONFIDENTIAL

WAR DIARY

of

6/7th Battalion, The Gordon Highlanders

For Period

1st January 1919   31st January 1919

VOLUME 50.

www.ingramcontent.com/pod-product-compliance
Lightning Source LLC
Chambersburg PA
CBHW081438160426
43193CB00013B/2319